中英文對照

道 德 經

（附楚简《太一生水》）

The Book of Tao and Teh

(With the Bamboo Slip-text：
"*The Great One Begot Water*")

辜正坤　譯

Translated by Gu Zhengkun

中国出版集团

中国对外翻译出版公司

图书在版编目（CIP）数据

道德经/(春秋) 老子著；辜正坤译. —北京：中国对外翻译出版公司，
2008.1

ISBN 978-7-5001-1200-6

Ⅰ. 道…　Ⅱ. ①老…②辜…　Ⅲ. ①英语—汉语—对照读物　②道家
Ⅳ. H319.4：B

中国版本图书馆 CIP 数据核字（2006）第 115696 号

出版发行 / 中国对外翻译出版公司

地　　址 / 北京市西城区车公庄大街甲 4 号物华大厦六层

电　　话 / (010) 68359376　68359303　68359101　68357937

邮　　编 / 100044

传　　真 / (010) 68357870

电子邮件 / book@ctpc.com.cn

网　　址 / http://www.ctpc.com.cn

策划编辑 / 张高里　李育超

责任编辑 / 李育超　薛振冰

封面设计 / 大象设计

排　　版 / 巴蜀阳光

印　　刷 / 保定市中画美凯印刷有限公司

经　　销 / 新华书店

规　　格 / 880×1230 毫米　1/32

印　　张 / 10

字　　数 / 300 千字

版　　次 / 2007 年 1 月第一版

印　　次 / 2013 年 7 月第五次

ISBN　978-7-5001-1200-6　　　　**定价：16.80 元**

Contents

目　録

《道德經》再版序
——郭店楚簡《老子》簡介

辜 正 坤

　　1993年,《老子》的最古的文本,或許也是迄今為止世界上曾經發現過的最早的書在中國發現!在湖北省沙洋縣紀山鎮郭店村發掘的古墓群中的一號墓中,出土了大量竹簡。考古學者們認定所發掘的古墓所在地應該是存在於公元前476年至前278年尚未被秦國所滅的楚國古都。一號墓建墓時間至遲應該是戰國中期偏晚(公元前4世紀至3世紀之間)。這些竹簡現在總稱為郭店楚簡。竹簡總數804枚,其中702枚為長簡,27枚為殘簡。簡上共書12072字。郭店楚簡的文本經恢復整理,分成18個部分,並釋讀為現代漢字,全部資料以《郭店楚墓竹簡》為書名由北京文物出版社於1998年5月出版。不用說,這些文本一經披露,立刻在中國乃至西方學術界引起軒然大波,一時議論蜂起,著述如潮。

　　這批竹簡最為特殊的地方,在於它們包含著儒道兩家經典文獻,歷時兩千三百餘年,其簡上文字居然奇跡般地安然無恙。其中的《老子》文本是迄今為止出土過的最古老的《道德經》文本,有的內容聞所未聞,有的文句與現存的通行版《道德經》,諸如王弼、河上公、嚴遵、馬王堆帛書老子等許多種版本的《道德經》文句有諸多異文。這批老子竹簡文獻分成三組或三個部分,分別命名為《老子甲》、《老子乙》和《老子丙》。但是在發現的道家文獻中最令人振奮的是有一篇從未聽說過的文本《太一生水》(以其文本中的第一句命名)。許多學者相信,這個文本是現存中國人關於宇宙成因的最古老的文獻。如果將這一部分也加入現存《老子》,則《老子》一書的長度會明顯增加,超過現有的81章。學者們

對《太一生水》是否屬於老子還無定論,但是我個人堅信這是《老子》的一部分。這是我將此部分收入本書的原因。

　　郭店楚簡《老子》中有若干異文觀點令人震驚,具有很大的學術意義。例如下述文句據信為郭店楚簡本《老子》中含義更動最大者,即通行本中的"絕聖棄智"和"絕仁棄義"仕郭店楚簡本中分別是"絕智棄辨"和"絕偽棄慮"。若干學者頗為興奮,認為由此可得出定論:老子並不真正反對"仁"這個觀念。他們並且推論,"絕聖棄智"和"絕仁棄義"這種觀念一定是後來的莊子及其門徒強加于《老子》文本的。既然郭店墓主同時收藏閱讀《老子》的文本和儒家文本,並且老子並不反對"仁",學者們都樂於認為儒道兩家當時並不勢同水火,至少並未有所衝突。對此,我还有一些別的看法,另文,不贅。

　　許多學者傾向于認為,郭店楚簡《老子》抄寫本及其下葬期最晚也晚不過公元前3世紀,其抄本理應早於下葬期,因此,有一件事是確鑿無疑的,這就是《老子》文本的產生勢所必然地至少早于戰國時期或在戰國早期。這樣一來,數十年來一些學者認為《老子》文本晚於《莊子》、《孟子》或《荀子》的看法是明顯錯誤的。

　　我的《道德經》譯本最初由香港新世紀出版社出版於1993年,之後經修訂由北京大學出版社出版於1995年,算起來前後重印過五次。我在翻譯本書時除了使用大家公認的大量老子《道德經》注釋本之外,也借鑒了馬王堆帛書《老子》。但是,鑒於郭店楚簡的《老子》文本是在1998年5月才由北京文物出版社出版的,因此未及將這一極其重要的考古成果反映在以前出版的譯本中。可喜的是,這次中國對外翻譯出版公司決定再版我的譯本,我於是借此機會對譯本進行了修訂。凡是在含義上與郭店楚簡《老子》有明顯出入的地方,基本上都參照郭店楚簡本做了補訂。為方便讀者查閱,將補訂的部分放在註腳中。此外,我還全文翻譯了"太一生水"這一道家文獻。儘管它是否是老子的本文,還無定論,但是其基本精神與老子的思想體系頗相呼應,則是無疑的。為了和現行《老子》相區別,《太一生水》全文附於後。

老子《道德經》英譯本自出版後,承蒙中外許多熱心讀者的關心,給我提出過許多寶貴的意見。美國莎士比亞協會會長David Bevington曾來函說,他認為我這個譯本是他所讀過的《道德經》譯本中可讀性最強的版本。一些國外的大學(包括美國耶魯大學)的教員曾使用過本書作為參考教材,這對譯者來說,都是 種鼓勵,成了本書第二次修訂的動力。中國對外翻譯出版公司李育超女士熱心提議再版此書,並提出若干修改意見,筆者都與此致以誠摯的謝意。

2006年8月譯者草於北京大學暢春園

Preface to the Second Edition of Book of Tao and Teh

——*A Brief Introduction to Guodian Slip-text of Lao Zi*

Gu Zhengkun

The year 1993 has witnessed an astonishing discovery of the earliest texts of *Lao Zi* in China, probably also the earliest book ever found so far in the world! In the village of Guodian, near the town of Jishan, the Shayang County, Hubei Province, lots of bamboo slips were unearthed in Tomb No.1 of the Guodian tombs. The archeological scholars confirmed that the place where the tombs were excavated was the ancient Chu capital from about 476 BC until 278 BC, before the State of Chu was overrun by the Qin Dynasty, and that the Tomb No. 1 was dated at least to the latter half of the Warring States period (mid 4th to early 3rd century BC). Those slips now are known as Guodian Chu Slips （郭店楚简）. The bamboo slips number in total about 804, including 702 strips and 27 broken strips with 12072 words. The Guodian Chu slip texts, being restored, were divided into eighteen sections, and have been transcribed into standard Chinese and published under the title *Chu Bamboo Slips from Guodian* by Cultural Relics Publishing House Publishing House, Beijing, May 1998. Needless to say, these manuscripts, once revealed, have given rise to great excitement in the intellectual community both in China and in the West, and they have brought

about a prodigious amount of scholarly controversies and output.

What is special about the slips is the fact that the texts written on strips of bamboo that have miraculously survived intact since 300 B.C. include both Taoist and Confucian classics. The text of *Lao Zi* is by far the earliest version of *Dao De Jing* ever unearthed. Some of the Taoist texts previously unknown or different from the received Taoist Texts, such as the texts edited by Wang Bi (王弼), He Shanggong (河上公), Yan Zun (严遵) and the *Silk Texts of Lao Zi* (帛书老子) found at Mawangdui (馬王堆) in 1973. The Taoist texts are divided into three parts, or three bundles, respectively called *Lao Zi (A)*, *Lao Zi (B) and Lao Zi (C)*. The extreme exiting part of the discovery of the Taoist texts is the text so far never known and now entitled "太一生水" (*The Great One Begot Water*) (just named after the first line of the text). The text is believed by many scholars to be the oldest existing writing on Chinese cosmology. If this part is added to the present version of *Lao Zi*, the book length considerably increases, containing more than 81 chapters. For my own part, although some scholars still have doubts about the authorship, I firmly believe this text is the expression of Lao Zi's Taoism, that is why I have entered this text into the present book.

Some variants in *Guodian Lao Zi* offer startling ideas that are believed to be of great academic significance. For example, the following phrases are supposed to be the most important changes in the text of *Lao Zi* where 绝圣弃智 and 绝仁弃义 are respectively replaced by 绝智弃辨 and 绝伪弃虑. Some scholars thus vehemently conclude that this is the firm proof that Lao Zi was not really against Benevolence (*Ren*仁) and that the ideas of discarding benevolence and rectitude (绝仁弃义) and discarding sages and wisdom (绝圣弃智) must have been just the ideas of Zhuang Zi and his disciples who later on imposed the ideas on the Taoist texts. Since Lao Zi's texts were read and collected

together with Confucian texts and since Lao Zi is believed not to be against *Ren*, some Chinese scholars feel ready to suggest that Taoism and Confucianism were not hostile to each other, at least they did not go into conflict in their time. I wrote an article to voice my different opinion of the argument to be published recently in a journal.

Many scholars tend to think that one thing is certain, that is, with the discovery of the Guodian Chu slips transcribed before 300 BC (the latest possible date of their burial), the transcription must have been earlier than the burial itself, and Lao Zi's texts therefore must have been made at least before or in the early period of Warring States. Thus the assumption once held by some scholars for scores of years that Lao Zi's texts are later than works bearing the names of Zhuang Zi, Mencius, and Xun Zi is obviously wrong.

My translation of *Book of Tao and Teh* was first published by New Century Publisher in 1993, and then, after some revision, published by Peking University Press in 1995, and up to now reprinted 5 times. My English version takes advantage of manifold accepted Chinese editions, above all, *Mawangdui Silk Texts of Lao Zi*, usually with profuse annotations. However, *Guodian Lao Zi*, as an extreme important archeological achievement, was not made available because it was not until May 1998 that *Chu Bamboo Slips from Guodian* was published by Wenwu Publishing House, Beijing. Fortunately, I could now avail myself of the opportunity to attempt a revision proposed by China Translation & Publishing Corporation. Emendations are carefully made wherever I found them obviously necessary compared with the *Guodian Lao Zi* texts. Most emendations appear as notes for the sake of convenience of the reader to distinguish the supplements from the old version. Besides, I have translated the full text of 太一生水 (*The Great One Begot Water*), a Taoist document, though scholars so far do not reach the final conclusion as to whether it is the

text by Lao Zi; it is safe to say that the dominant spirit of the text echoes that of Taoist system of thought. In order to differentiate the text *The Great One Begot Water* from the current version of *Dao De Jing*, I have attached it to the end of the book.

I'd like to express my gratitude to many readers who have kindly shown their favor for the *Book of Tao and Teh* and offered many of their valuable suggestions ever since it was published. Thanks go to Professor David Bevington, president of the Shakespeare Association of America, who once wrote to me kindly saying my version is "the most readable" of the editions of *Lao Zi* he has ever read. My thanks also go to certain instructors of a couple of universities (including the Yale University) or colleges that once designated the book as the reference textbook for their students, which surely has encouraged the translator to further this third revision of the book.

Last but not least, my gratitude goes to Miss Li Yuchao, director of the Copyright & Planning Department of China Translation & Publishing Corporation, for her generous proposal of bringing to fruition the revision of the present edition of the book.

August 2006, Peking University

老子思想體系概論
——初版序

辜正坤

老子其人

　　《老子》一書的作者和成書年代問題,迄今無定論。這方面最早的文字記載見於司馬遷的《史記》。《史記》比較客觀地記述了當時流行的説法:"老子者,楚苦縣歷鄉曲仁里人也,姓李氏,名耳,字聃,周守藏室之史也。"楚苦縣,楚國苦縣,即今河南鹿邑;周守藏室之史,指東周王朝掌管圖書的史官。據傳老子博聞強記,同時代人孔子亦曾向他請教過周禮。他晚年隱居,共活了160多歲(另説200多歲)。

　　然而司馬遷本人也無法肯定上述流行看法的可靠性,出於一種史家特有的客觀態度,他因此又羅列出有關老子其人的其他兩種説法。其一,"或曰:老萊子亦楚人也,著書十五篇,言道家之用,與孔子同時云。"其二,"自孔子死之後百二十九年,而《史記》周太史儋見秦獻公曰:'始秦與周合,合五百歲而離,離七十歲而霸王者出焉。'或曰儋即老子,或曰非也,世莫知其然否。"(《史記·老子韓非列傳》)。這樣一來,《老子》一書的著作權人就有了三個候選者:李耳、老萊子、太史儋。前二人均與孔子同時,春秋時人;後者則晚於孔子,戰國時人。有關老子其人及其成書年代的説法,西漢時代就已大成問題。然而有關這個問題的大規模探討,卻是二十世紀的事情。民國十一年,梁啓超就此撰文提出若干疑問,遂引發出一場學術大辯論,那場辯論的文章多達五十萬字,後來都收集在多卷本《古史辨》一書中。辯論的結果是誰也説服不了誰。這場辯論時起時伏,一直延續到現在。尤其在《老子》成書年代問題上,爭論尤烈。綜括起

來,大約有三種觀點:1)《老子》成書於春秋;2)《老子》成書於戰國;3)老子思想形成於春秋,然而《老子》一書則成於戰國。戰國説似曾一度占上風,但相反的説法也振振有詞。縱觀七十餘年的論戰,可以窺見掩蓋在這個問題背後的是儒道兩家理論孰先孰後的問題,並進而牽涉到哲學門派與當代政治方面的利害關係,因而更使論争保持在無偏見的純學術立場上,是很不容易的事情。這個問題的真正解決,或有賴地下資料的發掘。

饒有趣味的是,恰好在本書翻譯脱稿並出版的1993年,湖北荆門郭店一號墓出土了一部分《老子》竹簡,經專家后來考證,斷言老子(或其候選人李耳、老萊子)及其思想産生於春秋晚期,應該有一定的考古學依據。我當時在此序文中認爲"這個問題的真正解決,或有賴地下資料的發掘",想不到在當年就印證。不過關于竹簡的具體内容是在1998年5月以后才由北京文物出版社披露的。今借修訂之機,補注於此。

老子的思想體系

比之於孔孟學説,老子的思想體系更嚴密、系統、一致。全書雖只五千言,然而包容甚廣,不惟對哲學問題有系統論述,對社會、歷史、倫理、政治、軍事乃至修身處世之道,均有相應的闡發。哲學是老子思想的核心,"道"則是老子思想核心的核心。以"道"爲立論基礎,道學理論可分爲聯繫極爲緊密的四大部分:1)道體論;2)道法論;3)道知論;4)道用論。道體論是本體論,是老子的宇宙觀;道法論是方法論,是老子思想中最精彩的部分,也是中國古代辯證法論述的高峰;道知論是認識論,講人類如何才能體察把握無所不在的道本身;道用論則是道體論、道法論在社會、歷史、人生等方面的具體應用。

1.道體論

1.1 道是萬物乃至宇宙的本原

"有物混成,先天地生;寂兮寥兮,獨立不改,周行而不殆,可以爲天下母。吾不知其名,字之曰道。"(第二十五章)老子的道有四個特點。其一,先天地萬物而生,甚至先神、帝而生:"道沖……吾不知誰之子,象帝之先。"(第四章);其二,具備單一的永恒的性質("獨立不改");其三,無休止地運動着("周行而不殆");其四,萬物之本原("天下母")。

1.2 道産生萬事萬物

道不僅僅是本原,道還産生萬物:"道生一,一生二,二生三,三生萬物。"(第四十二章)"道沖而用之或不盈。淵兮,似萬物之宗。"(第四章)道不是一下子就生出萬物,而是經歷了一個漸進的演變過程,這個過程有點像細胞的有序裂變過程。關於一、二、三的解釋,可取《淮南子·天文訓》:"道始於一,一而不生,故分而爲陰陽,陰陽和而萬物生。"

1.3 道是物質性的

老子的道在最初的情形使人聯想起康德的星雲假説:"道之爲物,惟恍惟惚;惚兮恍兮,其中有象;恍兮惚兮,其中有物;窈兮冥兮,其中有精。其精甚真,其中有信。"(第二十一章)"有象"、"有物"、"有精"、"有信",不但"有"並且"甚真"。其物質性是無疑的。所以道也可以看作"有",客觀存在本身就是道。天下萬物生於道,道既然可以看作有,因而老子説"天下萬物生於有"(第四十章)。

1.4 道也是精神性的

然而老子的道又與康德星雲説有很大區别，因爲它同時又是精神性的："視之不曰微。此三者，不可致詰，故混而爲一。其上不皦，其下不昧，繩繩不可名，復歸於萬物。是謂無狀之狀，無物之象，是惟惚恍。迎之不見其首，隨之不見其後。"(第十四章)這裏説得明明白白:道是"不見"、"不聞"、"無狀"、"無物"的精神實體。所以道也可以看作"無"，天下萬物既可以生於道，自然也就可以生於無，正無怪乎老子又説"有生於無"(第四十章)了。

1.5 道體乃心物一體

道是精神性的，也是物質性的。這就把現代人(尤其是西方人)給弄糊涂了。現代人習慣於單向形式邏輯思維:此就是此，彼就是彼，不可能既是此，又是彼。因此，許多年來，哲學家們一直爭論不休，要麽把老子判爲唯物主義哲學家，要麽把老子判爲唯心主義哲學家。而在我看來，老子超乎二者之上，他既不唯物，也不唯心，而是唯道。如果硬要給他貼一個標籤，讓他成爲什麽主義者，那麽，我們不妨稱他爲唯道主義者。他的道，如我們以上的分析，是精神性和物質性的統一體，是有和無的統一體，或簡言之，是心物一體。對他來説，有和無本來就是同一道體(本體)在不同條件下的存在(或顯現)方式(這立刻讓人想起黑格爾的絕對精神的存在與顯現方式)。無可以生有("有生於無"，第四十章)，有也可以生無("有無相生"，第二章)。此可以轉化爲彼，彼也可以轉化爲此。

有和無之間的轉化有過程、有條件，這一點，老子也是明白的。例如他説"道生一，一生二，二生三，三生萬物"，就表明他知道"道"(無)不能一下就成爲萬物，還有一個一、二、三的有序過程。又例如他説:"合抱之木，生於毫末;九層之臺，起於累土;千里之行，始於足下。"(第六十四章)毫末成木，累土成臺，也表明他知道質與量之間亦有個轉化的過程。只是由於哲理性思辨的簡潔要求，老子不糾纏於有和無之間無限多的漸進演變環節，而是緊抓住宇宙現象的兩個極端：有和無(物質性和精神性)，並將這兩個極端統一於道。有無共體這種現象，對於現代人來説，或許是矛盾的，而對於老子來説，却没有矛盾：無是一種特殊形態的有，有也是一種特殊形態的無。由此推之，精神是特殊形態的物質，物質是特殊形態的精神。没有絕對的有，也没有絕對的無。無中有有，有中有無，有無相對，有無貫通。所以最堅硬的物質實體，分析起來，也是由無限多的"無"一樣的空隙構成的(分子、原子、質子……結構等)；最空虛的真空，若加以考察，也會發現其中充滿了物質(例如波，例如光，歸根結底，也是物質)。

1.6 道氣同根同行

有無、心物之間的轉化連接，宇宙本身的萬千現象的周流運行，靠什麼手段或媒介來實現呢?靠氣："萬物負陰而抱陽，冲氣以爲和。"(第四十二章)"陰"是陰氣，"陽"是陽氣，"和"則是陰陽二氣交感和合生成的和氣。道與氣雖在一定的程度上同根同源亦同流，但道還是不能等同於氣，道比氣更爲根本。因爲道在包容有無的同時，它還是一種規律，體現着有、無、氣的存在和運行方式。氣無所不在，則道無所不至。

氣既然與道同根，自然也與有無同根。道教把氣寫作炁，就是在昭示氣與無的關係。《淮南子》里講到天地產生之前，有一種混沌未分之氣，此氣分爲陰陽二氣，輕清者爲陽氣，升而爲天；重濁者是陰氣，下降爲地。這種混沌未分之氣可以説就是無，乃天地之始，所謂無中生有。又，前引二十一章中的"其中有精，其精甚真"的"精"即精氣，老子説根據它就可以認識萬物的開始("以閲衆甫")，也是道、氣、無同根生萬物的另一證據。

2.道法論

在方法論方面,老子的辯證思想極爲精彩,可以説代表著中國古典哲學的最高成就。由於老子的思想方法常常無視普通人(尤其是現代人)的單向邏輯思維習慣,也由於老子的表述所用的是韻文格言體,省掉了大量在他看來不言自明的論證論據,所以他的辯證觀念很容易被今天的我們看作是一種詭辯。實際上《老子》一書蘊涵的辯證思想正在千萬次地被許許多多的中外哲學家重復着。

2.1 自然而然之法

在老子看來,天地萬物的運行興道相依歸,人法、地法、天法、道法,法法相依相成,而最高的法則是無法,即一切順其自然的無爲大法。所以老子説:"人法地,地法天,天法道,道法自然。"(第二十五章)從有法歸於無法(自然之法),繞了一個圈,所謂"反者道之動"是也(第四十章)。自然之法相依相盪,萬物自生、自化、自成、自滅,循環往復,無窮無盡。有法與無法互爲因果,從一個角度看是法,從另一個角度看則爲非法,反之亦然。

2.2 對立統一法

老子看到"萬物負陰而抱陽"(第四十二章),矛盾存在於一切事物之中。矛盾的陰陽雙方結成對立統一的辯證關係,相互聯繫,相互對抗、相互依賴。一系列的對立概念出現在《老子》一書中:大小、高下、前後、進退、美醜、新舊、強弱、剛柔、有無、損益、陰陽、榮辱、得失、禍福、吉凶、難易、勝敗、興廢、盈虛、貴賤等等,等等。例如:"天下皆知美之爲美,斯惡矣;皆知善之爲善,斯不善矣,故有無相生,難易相成,長短相形,高下相傾,音聲相和,前後相隨。"(第二章)"曲則

全,枉則直,窪則盈,敝則新,少則得,多則惑。"(第二十二章)

2.3 否定之否定法

老子很清楚,矛盾的雙方一旦發展到極端,就總是要向相反的方向轉化,產生自我否定。"反者道之動"就是這一命題的最佳表述。"物或損之而益,或益之而損。"(第四十二章)"甚愛必大費,多藏必厚亡。"(第四十四章)"物壯則老。"(第五十五章)"兵強則滅,木強則折。"(第七十六章)"其政悶悶,其民淳淳。其政察察,其民缺缺。禍兮,福之所倚;福兮,禍之所伏。"(第五十八章)"反者道之動"中的"反"通"返"。故此句有兩解:1)向相反的方向發展是道的運動;2)道的運動是循環往復,總要回到原初狀態的。兩種解釋互相不矛盾,並可互相補充。

2.4 質量轉換法

老子注意到事物的轉化不但有一個由小到大、由低到高、由弱變強的過程,而且有一個量變引起質變的結果:"合抱之木,生於毫末;九層之臺,起於累土;千里之行,始於足下。"(第六十四章)"圖難於其易,爲大於其細。天下難事,必作於易;天下大事,必作於細。"(第六十三章)"毫末"由於量變而質變爲"木","累土"由量變而質變爲"臺"。這些例子雖不是特別貼切,但質量轉化的含義是顯而易見的。

由上可知,老子的最高大法是一切順其自然的無爲之法,以無法爲有法,視有法若無法。對立統一、否定之否定、質量轉換,近代哲學的三大辯證律,都可以在老子的哲學方法論——道法——中找到雛形。

3. 道知論

道知論是老子的認識論,即如何認知宇宙萬物的本原"道"。與現代人通過科學知識、實證方法探討世界萬物之謎的做法相反,老子認爲太多的知識反倒有礙於認知道和世界;他主張不斷地拋棄知識("爲道日損"見第四十八章),"絕聖棄智"(第十九章),"絕學無憂"(第二十章),只有將知識"損之又損"才能達到"無爲"的境界。爲此,老子提出兩個體察道的辦法,即"玄覽"法和"靜觀"法。嚴格地説這是一個方法的兩個過程,這裏爲了叙述上的方便,略加分論。

3.1 玄覽法

所謂玄覽法即洗清内心的雜念,使心靈深處明澈如鏡,從而具備體察精微之道的途徑與能力。《老子》第十章説:"滌除玄覽,能無疵乎?"帛書"覽"作"鑑",通"鑑";鑑,鏡也。故"玄覽"乃"清澈幽深的明鏡"之意,此處喻心如明鏡,一塵不染。《莊子·天道篇》:"聖人之心,静乎天地之鑑,萬物之鏡也。"《淮南子·修務訓》:"執玄鑑於心,照物明白。"《太玄童》:"修其玄鑑。"都是以鏡喻心。老子主張"滌除"内心深處的雜念,使心能明白無誤地觀照道體道法。那麽,什麽是雜念呢?一個是知識,一個是欲望。知識是一大堆概念體系,這些概念總是或多或少帶有偏見或偏差,它們可以在一定的程度上使我們獲得新知,但却在更多的場合使我們誤入歧途。文化本身就是一種有色眼鏡,會歪曲我們對世界的看法。欲望激動我們的身心,從而扭曲我們的感官和心智,使我們無法平心静氣、不偏不倚地考察世界。因此"滌除"雜念就必須去知、去欲,即"棄智"(第十九章)、"絕學"(第二十章)、"少私寡欲"(第十九章),甚至達到"無私無欲"(第三章)的境界。但是,只靠講理論是不能使人"無知無欲"的,必須使用種種切實的可以身體力行的方法,這種方法不是别的,就是練氣功的方法。實際上第十章主要就是在講練氣功所能達到的境界:"載營魄抱一,能無離乎?專氣致柔,能如嬰兒乎?滌除玄覽,能無疵乎?……天門開闔,能爲雌乎?"人們在練功的時候,必須身心合一,儘量使身體放鬆,有如嬰兒,然後排除一切私心雜念,進入一種虛靈境界。也可以意守身上某個穴位,例如意守丹田(上丹田即天門,下丹田即肚臍下三寸處,"爲雌",守靜之意),即可進入氣功態。在這種狀態下,心如止水明鏡,道本身才有自然顯示出來的可能性。(世傳老子是一位氣功師,我亦深信。根據我個人的長期研究、統計,《老子》一書中有三千六百餘字是氣功訣或涉及氣功,占全書總字數的百分之七十以上。關於這個問題,將另文闡述,茲不贅。)因此,玄覽法,與禪宗師神秀所謂"身是菩提樹,心如明鏡臺。時時勤拂拭,莫使有塵埃"([唐]惠能:《壇經》第六節)之修心法一脈相通。

(附注:"靜坐"這個詞英文通常譯作"Sitting in meditation"。我這里也沿用這個舊譯法,目的只是從俗,讓西方人易解。其實嚴格説來,西方人將"靜坐"譯成Sitting in meditation是錯誤的,容易引起誤解。英文單詞meditation指的是沉思、冥想。而漢語"靜坐"不論作爲道家還是佛家修煉方法,都和"沉思、冥想"沒有關系。其實這個詞表達的修煉含義剛好相反:即摒除雜念,盡可能不要思想。西方讀者必須記住:一個氣功修煉者靜坐時剛好就是要消除雜念,盡量不要陷入沉思,否則很難進入氣功態。)

3.2 静觀法

静觀法上承玄覽法。即心身儘量放鬆,並與天地合一,排除一切雜念,進入氣功態之後,静觀默察蕓蕓萬物之奧秘。静觀法強調一個静字:"致虛極,守静篤。萬物並作,吾以觀復。夫物芸芸,各復歸其根。歸根曰静,是曰復命,復命曰常,知常曰明。"(第十六章)玄覽、静觀二法,都是主張體察萬物,並非是用五官去感察萬物,甚至也不是單獨的心察萬物。"滌除玄覽"的目的,是驅除雜念,使之不成爲道進入心身的障礙,要真正悟道,須使心和整個身體都成爲認知工具,尤其是使身體成爲認知工具。普通人只用我們身體的一部分——眼、耳、口、舌等——來察知世界,老子認爲這些感官是靠不住的。體察天道只能靠無知無欲的身心的統一體。只要施行了玄覽、静觀法,則可以"不出户,知天下;不窺牖,見天道。其出彌遠,其知彌少。是以聖人不行而知,不見而名,不爲而成。"(第四十七章)一些學者因爲老子排斥感覺經驗,便將他的認識方法看作是唯心主義的,這其實是誤解。因爲老子的認識方法不僅有心得之法,更主要的是還有體會之法。心物一體,"唯道是從"(第二十一章),所以老子的認識方法不是唯物,也不是唯心,而是心物一體的唯道主義之法。

4.道用論

老子將其辯證哲學觀念應用於客觀的歷史、社會、人生,遂産生相應的一套人生觀、政治觀、社會歷史觀。下試簡要分論之。

4.1 人生觀

老子的人生觀,是一種自我克制的陰性人生觀,是老子哲學觀的具體表現。主要表現爲不争、節欲、處柔和知足。

4.1.1 不争

老子可能看到人類相互敵對争鬥而帶來的無窮禍患,因此極力宣傳"不争"的好處:"上善若水,水善利萬物而不争。處衆人之所惡,故幾於道……夫唯不争,故無尤。"(第七章)以水喻利而不争之理,形象、貼切。只要"不争",就居然可以達到道的境界,並能因此不犯過失,這對常人來説,確實是一種誘惑。應該説這種思想是非常辯證和深刻的,但由於老子在表述這類觀念方面總强調其可帶來的實際利益,就很容易讓人感到他的"不争"思想似乎只是一種"大争"的手段:表面上不争,骨子里依然是争。結果深刻的哲理被人視爲一種權詐之術。又如:"曲則全,枉則直,窪則盈。……夫唯不争,故天下莫能與之争。"(第二十二章)從辯證認識的角度看,確是字字珠璣,但因爲强調了"不争"可以使人成爲天下的强者,百川歸順的"百谷王",就形成更大的誘惑,反使人爲了達到稱王稱霸的目的而爭着來實踐這"不爭"之論,這恐怕是老子始料未及者。要做到不爭,就必須一貫的甘於謙恭"處下","不自是"(不自以爲是),"不自伐"(不自己夸耀),"不自矜"(不自高自大)(第二十二章),且去知,去欲,"去甚,去奢,去泰"(第二十九章)。從這個角度來看,"不爭"確是一種美德,人人都來實踐這一道德原則,當然可以天下太平。然而老子明白得很:人們不可能真正實踐他的這種道德原則:"吾言甚易知,甚易行。天下莫能知,莫能行。"(第七十章)因此,爲了使人們樂於踐行此道,不惜以能獲高位大利誘之。老子的苦心,亦可謂深矣。雖力倡無爲之論,但這却又是一種精心的策略式有爲。"不爭"的思想演變爲"和爲貴"的思想,成爲兩千多年來中華民族心理結構中的主要成分,這是值得重視的。

4.1.2 節欲

人生而有三欲:食慾、性慾、權欲。經後天生活而演變爲物慾、情慾、權欲。老子認爲要真正施行不爭之道,首須去掉人欲,所以反復倡導"無欲"之論。但他同時知道,"無欲"只是一種理想,絕難實現,於是在另一個地方又提出"寡欲":"見素抱樸,少私寡欲"(第十九章),算是一種折衷之法。

作爲一種哲學命題,老子哲學體系中的"無欲"論最容易受到攻擊。對現代人來說,欲望既然是生而有之的東西,可見是合於天道的東西,硬要將之去掉,豈不是逆天違道?另一方面,人生之有意義,就在於能合理地滿足欲望,將欲望連根除掉,人就不復爲人,甚至連低等動物也不如。然而,俯察塵世,人欲橫流,爭訟不息,人類輾轉挣扎於慾海之中不能自拔,這也確實是一個需要解决的大問題。鄙意,解决的辦法可以有多種,例如將欲望疏導、轉移、節制三法不同程度地交叉使用,却絕不可採取簡單的因噎廢食的辦法。那麽,老子是否就是想採取徹底根除欲望的辦法呢?倒也不然。漢語表義難免模糊,古漢語尤其如此。加之古人使用概念常常不精密,對概念多不加界定,結果一個概念常常有幾種解釋。老子的"無欲"、"去欲"、"不欲",都不是絕對的説法。對常人而言,老子"無欲"的本義只是要節制欲望,即"見素抱樸,少私寡欲"(保持樸素,減少私

慾)。節欲的目的則是要使人們返樸歸真("復歸於樸",見第十九章),使世風淳樸,少奸詐欺詐。如果老子真是要徹底根絕欲望,那麼他爲什麼還主張使人民"甘其食,美其服,安其居,樂其俗"(第八十章)呢?甘食、美服、安居、樂俗,不正是欲望的最佳滿足麼?第二十九章中的"去甚、去奢、去泰"正是此種節欲觀的注腳。所以,找以爲老于是即欲論者,而非絕的無欲論者。几從字面上理解老子的"無欲"説法並施加攻擊是不妥的。

然而作爲一種練氣功的手段,老子的"無欲"論却又確實具有根除欲望的含義。如前所述,練功者要進入氣功態,須將種種雜念"滌除"掉,而欲望(如物慾、權欲)生出種種慾念,干擾練功,所以須去欲。如能達到萬念俱灰的境界,練功效果最好。此外,練功意味着導氣、蓄氣、煉氣。精氣、元氣要足,須保持精不外泄,方能練精化氣,如動輒縱慾,則精儘必氣絕,爲練功之大忌。所以,要行"專氣致柔"(第十章)之道,亦必須去欲。

由此可見,老子的"無欲"論,應作兩解。對一般人而言,是節欲;對練功者而言,是儘可能去欲。不知道這一區別,勢必把老子簡單地視爲一個禁慾論者。

4.1.3 處柔

老子認爲弱小的東西最終會戰勝强大的東西:"天下之至柔,馳騁天下之至堅。"(第四十三章)"天下莫柔於水,而攻堅强者莫之能勝,其無以易之。弱之勝强,柔之勝剛,天下莫不知,莫能行。"(第七十八章)因此,在現實生活中應居於弱小一方。這與上文的不爭思想不僅一脈相承,而且更加保守;即不僅是不爭,還要進一步樹立甘居於下的思想:"大國者下流,天下之交也,天下之牝。牝常以静勝牡,以静爲下。故大國以下小國,則取小國;小國以下大國,則取大國。故或下以取,或下而取。"(第六十一章)以此類推,則知"貴以賤爲本,高以下爲基;是以侯王自謂孤、寡、不穀谷。此非以賤爲本耶?非乎?"(第三十九章)不但邏輯推理如此,客觀事物本身也提供不少例证:"人之生也柔弱,其死也堅强。草木之生也柔脆,其死也枯槁。故堅强者死之徒,柔弱者生之徒。是以兵强則滅,木强則折。强大處下,柔弱處上。"(第七十六章)老子深知物壯則老,物極必反,所以,即便明知自己處於雄强的地位,也要安於柔雌的地位:"知其雄,守其

雌";即便明知自己處於光亮的地位,也要安於暗昧的地位:"知其白,守其黑。"(第二十八章)

從辯證的觀點看,老子的處柔思想固然十分深刻,但是一味處柔守柔,却必定使人日趨消極。從積極干預人生、改善人生的入世思想看,尊柔無異於自暴自棄。另一方面,並非一切弱小的東西總會戰勝强大的東西。强弱之間的轉化是有條件的。一般説來,只有新生的暫時處於弱小的東西才會戰勝表面上强大而實際上已盛極而衰的東西。老子却無視轉化條件,只强調處柔,是有局限性的。

不過,在一個人與人之間互相傾軋争鬥的社會中,主張抑强扶弱,應該説更合於人的倫理原則,因此,處柔的提法從和平治世的策略來看,不僅具有歷史意義,也具有現實意義。它與非暴力主義和勿抗惡主義是一脈相通的。

4.1.4 知足

人類要想使自己真正達到不争、節欲、處柔的境界,以便獲得真正的幸福,有一個簡便的途徑,那就是明白知足常樂的道理:"知止可以不殆。"(第三十二章)"知足者富。"(第三十三章)"知足不辱。"(第四十四章)"禍莫大於不知足,咎莫大於欲得。故知足之足,常足矣。"(第四十六章)幸福是什麼?幸福就是一種自我滿足的感覺。獲得這種感覺的途徑有兩條。一條是通過外部刺激,例如最大程度地合理合法地滿足一個人的食慾、性慾、權慾的辦法來獲得;一條是通過内省、例如徹底明白幸福不過是一種自我滿足的感覺這個道理,因此儘可能少地依賴外部刺激而直接借助於理性的悟解而獲得那種感覺。也許,知足常樂的思想是人類關於幸福的最偉大的思想。很難説究竟是誰在人類歷史上第一個發現了它。但是,老子對這個思想的闡述是確切的、實實在在的。單是這一點,就足以使老子躋身於人類史上最偉大的思想家之列。

4.2 政治觀

正如老子的人生觀一樣,老子的政治觀是老子的道的貫徹和體現。所以,在一定的程度上,只要把老子的人生觀擴大,就會産生老子的政治觀。這種推導法,老子自己也明確陳述過:"修之於身,其德乃真;修之於家,其德乃餘;修之於鄉,其德乃長;修之於國,其德乃豐;修之於天下,其德乃普。故以身觀身,以家觀家,以鄉觀鄉,以國觀國,以天下觀天下。吾何以知天下然哉?以此。"(第五十四章)老了的政治觀曾引起近代思想家們的多方非難,茲僅就要者撮述,計有無爲、不尚賢、愚民、小國寡民等思想。

4.2.1 無爲

老子所謂政治上的無爲,並非是什麼也不做,而是儘可能順其自然地做,即儘可能少地干預人民的生活,儘可能少地發號施令:"是以聖人處無爲之事,行不言之教,萬物作而弗始。"(第二章)"吾是以知無爲之有益。不言之教,無爲之益,天下希及之。"(第四十三章)"故聖人云:我無爲而民自化,我好静而民自正,我無事而民自富,我無欲而民自樸。"(第五十七章)"是以,聖人無爲,故無敗;無執,故無失。"(第六十四章)正因爲無爲,才能"無爲而無不爲"(第四十八章)。照老子的觀點,如果統治者過分地想要管理控制人民及其生活,其結果是"天下多忌諱而民彌貧;民多利器,國家滋昏;人多伎巧,奇物滋起;法令滋彰,盜賊多有"(第五十七章)。因此,老子認爲最好的辦法是採取放任主義,政府只宜成爲一個形同虛設的空架子,不宜自作聰明地去爲人民製定種種方針政策,政策越多越容易壞事,反把天下管理壞了。這樣一來,一個政府好與不好,不在於其有很多"政績",而是相反,在於其没有什麼"政績":"太上,不知有之;其次,親而譽之,其次,畏之;其次,侮之;信不足焉,有不信焉! 悠兮,其貴言,功成事遂,百姓皆謂我自然。"(第十七章)什麼都不管,反倒能什麼都管好。這個問題涉及是行"自然法"還是"人爲法","自律"還是"他律"的問題。從這個意義上講,我以爲老子不僅是人類思想史上最早的無政府主義者之一,也可以算是市場經濟思想的最早的先驅者之一。不過,就當代人類社會現狀而言,理想的做法或許是以"自律"爲主,"他律"爲輔。全照老子的思想去做,是不現實的。

4.2.2 不尚賢

既然實行無爲政治, 就不需要一班謀臣術士來制定太多的方針政策以輔佐天子出令,所以無須"尚賢"。所謂賢者,多半是一些有學問、有才幹的人,老子要去知、去欲,這批人成爲主要的障礙,所以老子疾呼"不尚賢,使民不争;不貴難得之貨,使民不爲盜;不見可欲,使民心不亂……使夫智者不可爲也。爲無爲,則無不治。"(第三章)賢者推重知識,以智治國,老子認爲這正是國家治不好的根源:"民之難治,以其智多。故以智治國,國之賊;不以智治國,國之福。"(第六十五章)老子這種治國方針與當代社會試圖奉行的尊重人才、尊重知識的方針,可以説是水火不相容。從純理論上講,一切對立的治國方策如果分别貫徹始終,都是有利有弊,各有千秋的。但是,當人類社會已經完全知識化的時候,推行去知去欲、不尚賢的做法是很難行得通的。

4.2.3 愚民

不尚賢的結果必定是推行愚民政策,即"虚其心,實其腹,弱其志,强其骨,常使民無知無欲"(第三章);"古之善爲道者,非以明民,將民愚之。"(第六十五章) 要真正全面地理解老子這種愚民政策, 就必須考慮到老子關於幸福的看法。老子認爲幸福在於知足、節欲,而不在於無限制地縱慾。"智慧出,有大僞。"(第十八章)老子認爲由於人類知識的發達而帶來的社會生産力的發展和科學技術的進步並不能真正使人類從苦難中解放出來。對於老子來説, 知識本身或許還不是罪惡,但知識確實阻礙着人類去獲得真正的安寧與幸福。因此,我以爲老子的愚民政策並不是像某些批評家指責的那樣, 是一種純粹爲統治階級服務的統治權術。實際上老子是根本反對王權統治的, 所以一再主張無爲政治,反對統治階級干預人民的社會生活,反對法令滋彰的現象,反復闡述"我(統治者)無爲而民自化"(第五十七章)的道理。如前所述,在一定的意義上,我們可以説老子是一個無政府主義者,因此,説他在爲統治者出謀劃策,這是誤解了他,也是和他的整個思想體系明顯矛盾的。關鍵在於,現代人認爲"愚"是一種壞事,而老子卻認爲"愚"是一種福氣。所謂"愚民",即是要讓人返樸歸真,去知、節欲、除僞、近道,真正享受老子心目中的那種幸福,並不是爲了讓統治階級的江山固若金湯。實際上老子的思想既反壓迫,也反剥削:"朝甚除,田甚蕪,倉甚虚。服文彩,帶利劍,厭飲食,財貨有餘,是謂盜竽。非道也哉。"(第五

十三章)將四體不勤却財貨有餘的統治階級視爲強盜,這真是罵得痛快。"民之饑,以其上食稅之多,是以饑。民之難治,以其上之有爲,是以難治。民之輕死,以其上求生之厚,是以輕死。"(第七十五章)這裏的"上"可以説已經把矛頭直指帝王老爺,把飢餓、動亂等社會問題都歸罪於最高統治者,這在當時恐怕真需要一種大無畏的氣概才敢説出這樣的話。老子還警告統治者:"民不畏死,奈何以死懼之?"(第七十四章)如果統治者一味鎮壓人民,那麽:"民不畏威,則大威至。"(第七十二章)剝奪者必被剝奪,壓迫者必被壓迫;凡鎮壓人民者,就如代替木匠砍木頭一樣,"希有不傷其手者"(第七十四章)。所以,對於老子的愚民政策,不能望文生義地理解,而應聯繫其整個理論體系來加以辯證考察,否則,最易曲解了這位大思想家。

4.2.4 小國寡民

凡以智以力治國者,爲滿足其擴張性權欲,必搞兼併、搞集權、搞大一統、搞大國沙文主義。老子既然主張去知、節欲、無爲而治、使民自化,則勢必主張儘量弱化王權、分化王權,從而使人民得到自主權。所以,我認爲老子是中國歷史上最早最徹底的民權論者和反戰派。這一點我們可以從他的"小國寡民"(第八十章)的主張得到證實。小國寡民明顯針對廣土衆民而發。由於人智的進化,文化的發展,生產力的擴張,交通工具的改進,大國兼併興隨之而來的戰爭都成爲司空見慣的現象,老子極端反對這種現象,所以明確主張"小國寡民。使有什伯之器而不用;使民重死而不遠徙;雖有舟輿,無所乘之;雖有甲兵,無所陳之……鄰國相望,鷄犬之聲相聞,民至老死,不相往來"(第八十章)。由於國家小,人口少,人民能自食其力,自給自足。加之交通不便,與外界接觸不多,不受文明的污染;統治者不干涉人民的生活,社會秩序無須靠武力來維持,因此沒有苛捐雜稅,沒有兵荒馬亂,民風淳樸,人人都可以隨心所欲地甘食、美服、安居、樂俗,這種世外桃源般的生活恐怕不只是古人才向往的生活,就是二十世紀的今天,苦於競爭、污染、精神空虛的許多現代人,也未嘗不視之爲天堂中的樂園。小國寡民,如果能實現,可能並不是像一些社會學家所批判的那樣落後和無味,人類已經吃夠了廣土衆民所帶來的苦楚,國土再大,人口再多,也只是徒增統治者的威權,而人民需要的主要是自滿自足的感覺和安寧。小國寡民,或許在當代是一種空想,但未必就不會成爲新世紀人類的希望之一。

4.3 社會歷史觀

社會歷史觀是老子政治觀的進一步擴大。倡無爲、不尚賢、愚民、小國寡民諸政策,其主觀目的是要使人類返樸歸真,回到人人平等的結繩記事的原始社會狀態中去(第八十章),其客觀手段則既包括反壓迫、反剝削、反王權、反戰爭,也包括反欲望、反知識、反科學、反文明。老子的以道爲本的社會歷史觀是一種非常冷靜的氣功師兼哲學家的思考結果。老子看出,壓迫、剝削、王權、戰爭等不平等現象的根源存在於人類先天性的欲望和後天性的知識、科學之類的文明發展過程中。所以,要徹底掃除不平等現象,就必須從根本上做起,即反欲望、反知識、反科學、反文明。這種社會歷史觀是當代人很難接受的,容易被斥爲空想的因噎廢食的復古倒退觀。

另一方面,隨着人類文明的高度發展,尤其是隨着科學的日新月異的大躍進,人類社會自身的矛盾也相應激化,作爲個體的人與社會、與自然界之間的矛盾也日益難以彌合。"回到自然"曾一度成爲近代若干哲學家的口號。越來越多的思想家認識到,科學是一把雙刃劍,它極大地爲人類謀福利的同時,也對人類造成極大的損害。像任何事物一樣,科學的每一個發展過程中,利和弊總是孿生兄弟。問題在於,人類是否有能力使它的利永遠大於弊?如果對這一點沒有把握,那麼,重新估價、借鑑老子的社會歷史觀無疑是有現實意義的。

人們習慣於說老子的社會歷史觀是倒退的,從文明發展的角度看,這是對的。但是,如果從價值判斷的角度認爲"倒退"就是不好的、壞的,那麼這是老子所不能同意的。從老子的反文化立場看,返樸歸真誠然是一種倒退,但這種倒退是好的, 是有益於人類的, 惟有倒退可以使人類重新獲得失去的安寧與幸福。而如果我們從老子唯道主義立場看,"反者道之動",事物既可以是此,也可以是彼。因此,可以說返樸歸真既是退又是進,即從"大爲"的時代退到淳樸的

時代,從逆道的社會進到順道的社會。把原始的人人平等的社會看作最高級最美好的社會,則後來的愈益文明的社會都是退化的社會。欲望、知識、文化的退,意味着向更高層次的大道大德的進。就從人的生理演變過程看,也是如此:大腦方面的進化是以四肢的退化爲代價的;成人體格的增長壯大是以不斷失掉嬰兒狀態時的先天元氣爲代價的。人體是一種雙向演進的有機體,既退化又進化。如果不理解老子的這種辯證思維方式,我們很容易將他的思想簡單化,斥之爲保守、落後、反動。

在我看來,人類社會今天面臨的苦惱,不是應不應該返樸歸真,而是發現自己已經再也沒有能力返回自然。因此,老子的社會歷史觀只能是一種理想,一種極其深刻的哲學思考。它或許能啓發當代人設法延緩某些社會進程,從而延緩人類自身的某些退化過程。

但是,人類的命運是人類自己的選擇造成的,哲學家的看法永遠只是一種忠告——並且經常是一種無用的忠告——我們還是讓人類自己去選擇吧,也許,從唯道主義的立場看,這正是一種順其自然、合於天道的態度。

關於本書的翻譯

《老子》一書的版本、注譯本,多得不可勝計。毋庸諱言,拙譯曾參考過大量的相關資料(見書末附參考書目)。在很多場合,當有若干種異文需要加以甄別與選擇時,譯者總是在細心比較了各種新舊版本之後,儘可能擇善而從。然而仁者見仁、智者見智,我之所謂善者,別人未必以爲盡善。好在有關老子的參考書極多,讀者可參照校讀,如發覺拙譯亦有可取處,則譯者就深感萬幸了。

此外,應一些外國朋友的請求而加注拼音,目的是爲了讓不會漢語的人也能讀《老子》。《老子》一書原爲詩體,現在讀起來,很多地方不協韻,其中一個重要原因是古音經過兩千多年的衍變,和今音已大不相同。其中有若干古字讀音,現已不可稽考。爲當代讀者(尤其是外國學習漢語的讀者)着想,本書注音一般

按現代讀音拼注。個別通假字按實際讀音注。

　　要將《老子》這樣一部具有世界意義的哲學名著譯成英語,其難度是可想而知的。這裏除了要感謝我在聯合國教科文組織總部(巴黎)及英美各國的朋友和有關學者外,首先要感謝我從前的博士導師李賦寧先生,沒有他的諄諄教誨,這個譯木是難以產生的。其次是澳大利亞專家Tony Gallagher博士,謝謝他仔細訂正了我的英語前言中的若干不妥之處。最後,在本書的翻譯過程中,胡雙寶、張文定二位先生提出了許多寶貴的意見,周學藝先生對英文稿提出了若干有益的建議,我的夫人趙宏通讀清樣數遍,雅意勤勤,譯者於此均致以謝忱。

　　　　　　　　1993年9月初稿於法國巴黎

　　　　　　　　聯合國教科文總部

　　　　　　　　1994年5月定稿於

　　　　　　　　北京大學英語系

　　　　　　　　2006年8月修訂於

　　　　　　　　北京大学英語系

LAO ZI AND HIS PHILOSOPHICAL SYSTEM

An Introduction

Gu Zhengkun

Lao Zi the Man

The authorship and date of *Lao Zi* (*Lao Tzu*) (also called *The Book of Tao and Teh*, *The Book of Tao Teh Chin or The Book of Lao Zi*) has been hitherto debatable. The earliest record of the issue is seen in *Recordings of History* by Sima Qian (145 BC—?BC), which contains a relatively objective version of the statement believed by Sima Qian's contemporaries that "Lao Zi once lived in Qurenli of the town of Lixiang, the Ku County, the State of Chu. His family name is Li, his personal name is Er, with the cognomen Dan. He was head of the imperial library of the Eastern Zhou Dynasty (770 BC—256 BC)." (Sima Qian, *Recordings of History*, China Bookshop, Beijing, 1980, PP. 2139—2143.) The Ku County of the State of Chu now is called the Luyi County of Henan Province. It is said that Lao Zi read widely and had a striking memory and that Confucius, his contemporary, once asked him for advice on the rites of the Zhou Dynasty. His later years were lived in seclusion; and he was believed to have a life-span of more than 160 years (or more than 200 years as some others conjectured).

But even Sima Qian himself was not sure of the reliability of the statement above; it was only out of an objective attitude peculiar to a historian that he recorded for reference the other two statements: 1) "Some one says, a man called Lao Laizi was also a native of the State of Chu, who wrote a book with a length of 15 chapters, discussing the use of Taoism and he was one of Confucius' contemporaries"; 2) "129 years later after the death of Confucius, it was recorded in a history book that Zhan, an imperial historian of the State of Zhou, once said to Chin Xian-gong, the Lord of the State of Chin: 'In the beginning, the State of Chin and the State of Zhou were united into one and kept in order for five hundred years until they finally separated from each other. After seventy years of separation, there came into being a conqueror.' Some says, Zhan is Lao Zi, but some others say no. Nobody has so far been sure of the matter." (See Sima Qian, *Recordings of History*.) Thus the authorship of *The Book of Lao Zi* involves three candidates: Li Er, Lao Laizi and Zhan the imperial historian. The former two were Confucius' contemporaries in the period of Spring and Autumn while the last one lived in the period of Warring States, later than the time of Confucius. From this, one can see clearly that the statements about the authorship of *The Book of Lao Zi* and the time at which it was written presented big problems even in the period of the Western Han Dynasty. But it was not until the twentieth century that probing into the issue on a fairly large scale has been taken seriously. In 1922, an article written by Liang Qichao posed many questions about it and gave rise to a great academic debate. The result of the polemical war was a multi-volume book of five hundred thousand words entitled *New Insight into Ancient Facts* in which articles involving the debate were all included. As is usually the case, there was no winner in the war. The debate, with ups and downs, has continued up to now. The focus of the debate has been on the date of *The Book of Lao Zi*. In general, three points of view are popular: 1) the book was written in the period of Spring and Autumn; 2) the book was written in the period of Warring States;

3) although the book was written in the period of Warring States, the ideas of Lao Zi took shape in the period of Spring and Autumn. The second view seems to have prevailed for a time, but the other two, backed by their own facts, have never shown any sign of losing their eloquence. Viewing the debate in perspective spanning more than seventy years, one is apt to awaken to the secret underlying the issue: the essential part of the debate is concerned with the problem of priority of Confucianism to Taoism or vice versa. Further, the debate inevitably invokes sectarian bias among philosophical schools and very often is subtly influenced by contemporary political considerations. Therefore, to keep the debate on a purely academic plane is almost an illusion. It seems to me the true solution to the problem does not lie in the continuing war of words between scholars on earth but lies underground, that is, the underground cultural relics to be excavated. So let's stop here and proceed to discuss what is more important: the Taoist system of Lao Zi.

(Author's note: It is interesting to say that my casual assertion that the true solution to the problem of the dates might lie in underground cultural relics to be excavated should have been corroborated right in the same year 1993 when my translation of *The Book of Tao and Teh* came into print, because part of *Lao Zi* on bamboo slips was unearthed in No.1 tomb in the Guodian village near the city of Jinmen, Hubei province at the end of that year! The textual research made by some experts confirmed that there is some archaeological reason to say that Lao Zi (or other two candidates Li Er and Lao Laizi) and his philosophy (at least in part) belong to the late period of Spring and Autumn. Fortunately, in May of 1998, the details of the Guodian Chu Slips were revealed to the public by Cultural Relics Publishing House, Beijing. Now I am happy to avail myself of the opportunity of revising the book to give a note here.)

The Taoist System of Lao Zi

Compared with Confucianism preached by Confucius and Mencius, Lao Zi's Taoism is more systematic, more prudent and more coherent. Containing only about 5,000 characters, *The Book of Lao Zi* covers subjects comprehensively ranging from philosophy, history, politics, ethics, to cultivation of man's mind. Philosophy is the chief concern of Lao Zi's thought with Tao as its core. Centering around that core, Taoism is systematically constructed with four integral parts: 1) Tao as the ontological being; 2) Tao as the dialectic law; 3) Tao as the epistemological tool; 4) Tao as a practical guide to worldly affairs. Tao as ontological being forms the essential of Lao Zi's outlook upon the world; Tao as the dialectic law embodies Lao Zi's methodology; Tao as the epistemological tool explains how mankind can approach the Taoist being; while Tao as a practical guide to worldly affairs means its specific application to explaining society, history, life and so on.

1 Tao as Ontological Being

1.1 *Tao is the origin of all things and the universe*

"There is a thing integratedly formed / And born earlier than Heaven and Earth. / Silent and empty, / It relies on nothing, / Moving around for ever. / We may regard it as the mother of all things. / I do not know its name. / So I name it as Tao."(Ch. 25) Notice should be taken of the four features of Tao: 1) Tao is born prior to the formation of heaven and earth, even prior to God;

"Tao is invisibly empty... / I do not know where it comes, / It seems to have appeared / before the existence of God"(Ch. 4); 2) Tao is of a unique and independent nature: "it relies on nothing"; 3) Tao is always on the move: "Moving around for ever"; 4) Tao is the origin of all things and the universe: "the mother of all things"; "Tao... is profound like the originator of all things" (Ch. 4).

1.2 *Tao begets all things*

Tao is the mother of all things, thus it begets all things: "Tao begets the One; / The One consists of the Two in opposition (the Yin and Yang); / The Two begets the Three; / The Three begets all things of the world."(Ch. 42) Tao does not beget all things at the same time but undergoes a gradual evolutionary process, very much resembling the process of an orderly fission of a cell, or resembling the natural result of the marriage of male with female. The relatively sound explanation of the One, the Two and the Three is believed to be found in "On Astronomy" in *Huai Nan Zi*: "The Tao begins with the One; the One cannot beget itself, thus it separates as the Yin and the Yang. When the Yin and the Yang intermingle into perfect harmony, all things gradually come into being."

1.3 *Tao is materialistic*

The primary condition of Tao reminds us of Kant's hypothethes of nebular; Lao Zi says, "The forms of the great Teh (virtue) / Exclusively depend on Tao. / Tao as a thing is vague and indefinite, / Vague and indefinite, / It presents images; / Indefinite and vague, / It embodies substance. / Distant and dark, / It embraces semen-like essence. / The essence is a genuine existence / That can be tested as true." (Ch. 21) Words like "images", "substance", "essence", "genuine existence", and "tested as true" obviously indicate the materialistic nature of Tao. Therefore, it is reasonable to regard Lao Zi's Tao as the substantial Being; or in other words, the objective world itself is the Tao. All things in the world are born from Tao and Tao is Being; that is why Lao Zi says, "All things of the world are born from Being". (Ch. 40)

1.4 *Tao is also spiritual*

Tao is, after all, chaos-like, greatly different from the nebular suggested by Kant, for it is at the same time spiritual: "What cannot be seen is called the 'Yi' (without colour); / What cannot be heard is called the 'Xi' (without sound); / What cannot be touched is called the 'Wei' (without shape). / These three things can be in no way defined, / So they are combined into one. / Above it there is no light; / Below it there is no darkness; / So vague as to defy any description. / It is categorized as nothingness, / And is called the shape without shape / As well as the image without substance. / It is hence named as 'Huhuang' (vague and dimly visible). / Facing it, you cannot see its front; / Following it, you cannot see its back." (Ch. 14) Words like "cannot be seen", "cannot be heard", "cannot be touched", "the shape without shape", "the image without substance" and "nothingness" obviously indicate the spiritual nature of Tao, therefore, it is also reasonable to regard Tao as the spiritual Being, or in other words, Tao itself is Nothingness. Since all things of the world are born from Tao, it is equally natural to say that they are born from Nothingness, that is why Lao Zi says, "All things of the world are born from Being. / And Being from Nothingness." (Ch. 40)

1.5 *The ontological Tao is the combination of the spiritual and the materialistic*

The duality of Tao as both the spiritual and the materialistic surely puzzles modern (especially Western) minds. Modern people are used to the one-way thinking fettered by formal logic: A is A just as B is B; nothing can be both A and B at the same time. For centuries, philosophers have been arguing over the question whether Lao Zi is a materialist or an idealist. To me, Lao Zi is neither of the two; he is above both. If one feels Lao Zi must be labelled as some sort of-ist, we can, as many other philosophers have been doing, simply call him a Taoist. His Tao, as we have stated above, is the combination of the spiritual and the materialistic, of mind and matter, or, of the substantial Being and Nothingness. With Lao Zi, the substantial Being and Nothingness are different forms of existence (or display) of the ontological Tao under different conditions. This immediately reminds us of the way in which Hegel's Absolute exists and exhibits. Nothingness can beget Being (Ch. 40: "... and Being from Nothingness"); Being can beget Nothingness (Ch. 2: "Hence Being and Nothingness beget each other". The original sentence, when translated word for word, is "Being and Nothingness beget each other.") Thus we are told that A can be converted into B, and likewise, B can be converted into A.

Of course, Lao Zi also understands that the conversion between Being and Nothingness must undergo a process of conditional change. He knows that Tao (Nothingness) cannot beget all things in the world once and for all; instead, there must be an orderly process from one to two, three... etc. That is why he says, "Tao begets the One; / The One consists of the Two in opposition (the Yin and the Yang); / The Two begets the Three; / The Three begets all things of the world." (Ch. 42) In another place, he states, "A huge tree grows from a tiny seedling; / A nine-storey terrace rises from a mound of earth; / A journey of a thousand li / Starts from beneath one's feet.Ch. 64) It is obvious that Lao Zi clearly recognizes the necessary process of conversion between quality and quantity; it is only out of a consideration of the philosophical brevity in expression that he avoids being involved in describing the countless links of gradual evolution between Being and Nothingness. He wisely gets hold of the extremes of universal phenomena: the substantial Being and Nothingness (the materialistic and the spiritual); and further, he unifies these two extremes into Tao. It may sound self-contradictory to modern people to say that Being and Nothingness are the same thing, but, to Lao Zi, there is no contradiction at all: Nothingness is the special form of the substantial Being while Being is the special form of Nothingness. Similarly, mind is the special form of matter while matter is the special form of mind. There is neither the absolute Being nor the absolute Nothingness. Nothingness exists in Being just as Being exists in Nothingness. Being and Nothingness exist in opposition as well as permeate each other. Therefore, the hardest matter, if being analyzed closely, will be found to be of a nature of countless Nothingness-like structures such as molecules, atoms, protons; the most empty vacuum, if being closely examined, will be found to be full of matter such as waves, light, gravitational force.

1.6 *Tao and Qi originate from the same root and move along the same route*

The connection and conversion between Being and Nothingness as well as the operation and movement of the myriad things of the world are realized by a means and medium called Qi: "All things connote the Yin and the Yang; / And

the Yin and the Yang keep acting upon each other / And thus things keep changing and unifying themselves."(Ch.42.) Here "Yin" means the Yin Qi (the female or negative Qi); "Yang", the Yang Qi (the male, or positive Qi). Tao and Qi, though, to some extent, of the same root and origin, are, after all, not exactly the same thing. Tao is more essential than Qi. Tao embodies both Being and Nothingness, and meanwhile, it functions as a law underlying the way in which Being, Nothingness and Qi exist and operate. Qi is full of the universe, thus Tao is found everywhere.

Since Qi shares the same origin with Tao, it naturally shares the same root with Nothingness. In certain Taoist books, the character Qi (氣) is spelled almost exactly as the character Nothingness (炁), evidently indicating the close relationship between Qi and Nothingness. The book *Huai Nan Zi* talks about a sort of Qi in chaos before the formation of Heaven and Earth. Qi consists of Yin and Yang; the light Qi is of the nature of Yang, going up on high and turning into Heaven while the heavy Qi is of the nature of Yin, falling down and turning into Earth. The sort of Qi is, so to speak, Nothingness, the beginning of Heaven and Earth. It is, in other words, what Lao Zi calls "Being born from Nothingness." Again, in Chapter 21, we read:"It embraces semen-like essence. / The essence is a genuine existence / That can be tested as true." Here the "semen-like essence"is the very Qi, "within which,"as Lao Zi says, "the beginning of all things can be surveyed." Thus we know Tao, Qi and Nothingness are of the same origin and combine to beget all things of the world.

2 Tao as the Dialectic Law

Methodologically, Lao Zi's dialectic ideas, so impressive and wonderful, are often said to mark the peak of classical Chinese philosophy, though they are, on the other hand, occasionally discarded as a sort of sophistry, chiefly because Lao Zi ignores the conventional, one-way logical mode of reasoning, omits lots of what he deems self-evident arguments in his theory, and what is more, the verse-form of his maximal lines sometimes also serves to be a hindrance to a correct understanding of his thought. Today, few philosophers will deny the fact that Lao Zi's ideas have been repeated by many thinkers at home and abroad.

2.1 *The law of nature*

According to Lao Zi, there are various laws underlying all things of the universe including Heaven, Earth, and Man; however, the best and the most functional laws are those which are most natural, or, in other words, are those which completely follow the Tao (Way) of Nature, thus he says, "Man takes Earth as his model; / Earth takes Heaven as its model; / Heaven takes Tao as its model; / Tao takes what is natural as its model." (Ch. 25) Obviously, we have followed Lao Zi in a circle starting from the law of man, through the laws of Heaven, of Earth, of Tao, to the anti-law of nature (without law): "Cycling is the movement of Tao." (Ch.40) The law and the anti-law are inter-dependent; viewed from this angle, the law is law; from that angle, no law at all!

2.2 *The law of the unity of opposites*

Lao Zi understands "All things connote Yin and Yang" (Ch. 42). Contradictions are universal. The two opposite sides are by no means isolated but are mutually interdependent. A lot of contradictory concepts in pairs thus frequently appear in *The Book of Tao and Teh*: big and small, high and low, advance and retreat, beautiful and ugly, new and old, strong and weak, rigid and supple, having and having-not, honor and disgrace, gain and loss, Yin and Yang, difficult and easy, etc. Several concepts are cited in Chapter 2, for example: "The whole world knows the beautiful as beautiful / Hence the existence of the ugly; / The whole world knows the good as good / Hence the existence of the bad. / Therefore existence and Nothingness beget each other; / Difficult and easy complement each other; / Long and the short manifest themselves by comparison; / High and low are inclined as well as opposed to each other; / Musical sound and singing voice harmonize each other; / Front and back follow each other." The concepts also appear in Chapter 20: "Bow down and you are preserved; / Bend and you can be straight; / Hollow, then full; / Worn, then new; / Seek a little and you get a lot; / Seek a lot and you get perplexed."

2.3 *The law of negation of negation*

Lao Zi knows well that extremes meet. The two opposite sides in a contradiction develop and finally transform into their opposites; modern scholars often refer to this as the Law of Negation of Negation. Lao Zi also clearly puts it in another way: "Cycling is the movement of Tao" (Ch.40); "A thing is sometimes added to when being reduced, / Or is reduced when being added to"(Ch. 42); "Excessive meanness will result in great expense; / Too much amassment leads to great loss"(Ch. 44); "A creature in its prime / is at the turning-point of being old"(Ch. 55); "the army, having grown strong, will be wiped out, / And the tree, when grown up, will be cut down"(Ch. 76); "Disaster hides itself behind good fortune; / Good fortune leans against disaster"(Ch. 58).

2.4 *The law of conversion between quality and quantity*

Lao Zi notices not only the process of things changing from the small into the big, from the weak into the strong, but also the result of the conversion between quality and quantity. "A huge tree grows from a tiny seedling; / A nine-storey terrace rises from a mound of earth; / A journey of a thousand *li* starts from beneath one's feet"(Ch. 64); "The big stems from the small; / The many is based on the few. / To overcome the difficult should begin with the easy; / To accomplish what is big should begin with the small. / The difficult things in the world must originate in the easy; / The big things in the world must take root in the small. / That is why the sage can accomplish what is great by never attempting to be great."(Ch. 63) The change from "a tiny seedling" into "a huge tree" and from "a mound of earth" into "a nine-storey terrace" surely suggests not only the quantitative nature of things in their course of development, but also a change of a qualitative nature.

It is, therefore, very interesting to know that the three great laws of dialectics characterizing modern philosophy find their embryonic forms in Lao Zi's Taoism, which, we must remember, take the law of nature as the highest principle that everything has been observing ever since the birth of the world.

3 The Taoist Epistemology

Totally different from the epistemological method characterizing modern philosophy that is somewhat intended to be scientific and pragmatical, Lao Zi's Taoist epistemology is mainly based on the discard of knowledge, the suppression of desire and, most important of all, on the bodily perception of the truth of the universe. Lao Zi insists that knowledge prevents man from knowing the world, so he maintains, "He who seeks Tao must reduce his knowledge every day"(Ch. 48); "Discard cleverness and wisdom / And the people will benefit themselves a hundredfold... / Discard cultural knowledge and worries will disappear."(Ch. 19) In order to really understand and gain Tao, Lao Zi suggests that two approaches to Tao be taken: the meditative approach and the keeping-to-stillness approach. Strictly speaking, these two approaches are the two stages of the same cognitive process. Sometimes, they are actually one thing. I now discuss them separately only for the sake of convenience of narration.

3.1 *To approach Tao through a deep meditation*

Lao Zi teaches that deep meditation helps man a lot in perceiving the truth of the world, Tao. A successful meditation needs to get rid of one's distracting thoughts. Distracting thoughts stem from knowledge and desires. Knowledge is a chaotic system of concepts and ideas which are indubitably biased. Knowledge helps us a lot just as it misleads us on many occasions. Culture itself functions as colorful glasses distorting our view of the physical world. Desires excite our

bodies and befuddle our mind, distorting our senses and reason, rendering us unable to observe and examine the world calmly and objectively. A deep meditation, therefore, summons up the great necessity of discarding knowledge and desires. "Keeping the people from knowledge and desires"(Ch. 3); "Discard cleverness and wisdom / And the people will benefit themselves a hundredfold... keep being simple in nature and mind, / Discard selfishness and weaken desires. / Discard cultural knowledge and worries will all disappear"(Ch. 19). Of course, one cannot easily get rid of knowledge and desires by purely exposing oneself to theoretical persuasion. There must need some means that are both practical and applicable. Sitting in meditation, for example, is one of those means; or more popularly, people call it the art of Qigong (breathing exercises)." Body and soul are one, / But can they avoid separation? / Concentrating on breathing exercises to be supple, / Can you become as supple as a baby? / Though you can get rid of your distracting thoughts for a deeper meditation, / Can you be devoid of blemish?"(Ch. 10) As is known, when we are engaged in breathing exercises, we must try our best to relax ourselves, entering into a spiritual state. Or we may also concentrate our mind on certain vital point on our bodies, say, keeping in mind the *Dantian* (a point in the center of the body; it is located roughly two inches below the navel and deep within the pelvis, and is usually named *Dantian* to indicate a vital center of Qi) with body and mind being in perfect harmony and all distracting thoughts removed. If we practice in this way for a few months, we can gradually sense the presence of Qi at the *Dantian* point in the form of localized warmth or heat. Thus we can enter the Qigong state in which our hearts are like "still water and flawless mirror" that can reflect Tao itself and we thereby perceive the truth of Being and the whole world.

　　(Note: In the West, "sitting in meditation" is a popular translation of the

Chinese term 静坐. I use the old expression for the convenience of making myself understood by Westerners. Strictly speaking, the term is mistranslated and thus misleading. As we know, meditation in English suggests deep thinking or pondering, while 静坐 in Chinese, both as a Taoist and Buddhist practice, does not mean anything like meditation at all. Rather, it just means the opposite: without thinking or thinking of nothing. Western readers need to remember what a Qigong practitioner intends in 静坐 is to get rid of his distracting thoughts, trying hard not to fall into meditation, or he is unable to enter into the Qigong state.)

3.2 *Observation by keeping to stillness*

The keeping-to-stillness approach is actually a necessary step toward deep meditation. Let a complete quietude control us, let Heaven, Earth and Man be in perfect harmony, and all distracting thoughts troubling our mind will be gone: thus we can calmly observe the secrets of all things. Stillness is essential to this approach. "I try my best to be in an extreme emptiness of mind; / I try to keep myself in a state of stillness. / From the vigorous growth of all things / I perceive the way they move in endless cycles. / All things, full of vitality, / Finally return to their own roots. / Returning to roots means stillness, / Also means a return to destiny."(Ch. 16) Only by keeping oneself in a state of stillness can one be in a position to see the images of truth itself. What characterizes the deep meditation and quiet observation is a unique idea that we should not merely rely upon our reason and organs of sense such as eyes, ears, nose; rather, we should perceive the whole being by employing our whole body as a cognitive tool to grasp Tao, hence our bodies are bodily tools of perception. Our organs of sense and reason are far from being reliable because they are, in most cases, in the bondage of knowledge and desires. This does not show, however, that Lao Zi absolutely excludes the use of reasoning power on the part of human beings; the philosopher actually preaches that it is the very unity of body and mind as a whole devoid of knowledge and desires that provides mankind with a supreme state in which Tao is most clearly perceptible. According to Lao Zi, the quiet observation and deep meditation enables a Taoist to know everything: "Without stirring out of the house, / One can know everything in the world; / Without looking out of the window, one can see the Tao of Heaven. / The further one travels, / The less one knows. / That is why the sage / Knows everything without going out; / Sees the Tao of the world / without looking out of the window." (Ch. 47)

Some scholars tend to think that Lao Zi's Taoist epistemology is idealist because Lao Zi excludes sensual experiences. This is only a matter of understanding. Lao Zi's cognitive mediums include both mind and body. Mind and body are one. Thus we say right at the beginning that Lao Zi is neither a materialist nor an idealist but an out-and-out Taoist who, in terms of Lao Zi's own Taoism, is a man of great Teh, "exclusively depend on Tao." (Ch. 21)

4 Tao as a Practical Guide to Worldly Affairs

Lao Zi applies Tao to the explanation of history, society and life, offering a system of views which later on, to a considerable degree, function as models on which classical Chinese politics, economy and culture are fashioned. What follows is a brief introduction to his system.

4.1 *An outlook upon life*

Lao Zi's view of life is completely negative, self-restrained, a living embodiment of his philosophy. It is characterized by a) anti-competition; b) moderation of desire, c) preference for the weak and d) self-contentment.

4.1.1 *Anti-competition*

Possibly having painfully witnessed a world of injustices and troubles caused by hostilities among mankind, Lao Zi advocates the advantages of anti-competition: "The perfect goodness is like water. / Water approaches all things / instead of contending with them. / It prefers to dwell where no one / would like to stay; / Hence it comes close to Tao. / A man of perfect goodness / chooses a low place to dwell as water, / He has a heart as deep as water, / He offers friendship as tender as water, / He speaks as sincerely as water, / He rules a state as orderly as water, / He does a thing as properly as water, / He takes action as timely as water. / Like water, he never contends with others, / So he never commits a mistake." (Ch. 8) It is surely a great temptation for common people to be led into the paradise of Tao by only observing an anti-competition approach. Philosophically speaking, we feel compelled to acknowledge the profoundity of the idea of anti-competition in historical perceptive, but when the idea is expressed with an emphasis on its advantages, one can be left with the impression that the philosopher's anti-competition only serves as a means of being a winner in great competition: anti-competition in words, great competition in deeds. As a result, the idea has been often regarded as a sort of political trickery.

Similarly in Chapter 22, Lao Zi says, "Bow down and you are preserved;

/ Bend and you can be straight; / Hollow, then full; / Worn, then new; / Seek a little and you get perplexed. / Thus the sage adheres to this One principle (Tao) / And regards it as the pattern of all things. / Show off yourself not and you become conspicuous; / Regard yourself not as infallible / and you become illustrious; / Brag about yourself not / and you gain achievement; / Boast of yourself not / and you become a head. / One does not contend with others, / So nobody in the world can win him in contention. / The ancients' saying 'Bow down and you are preserved' / Is surely not an empty saying / Which can be really proved effective."(Ch. 22) Again the promise that anti-competition can otherwise lead to a state in which one can become "the king of all valleys" seems for man a greater temptation. This may not have been Lao Zi's original intention. Nevertheless, for more than two 2,000 years, countless kings, lords or so-called heroes in China have been making use of this trick-like principle in order to realize their ambitions. Anti-competition means "show off yourself not", "brag about yourself not", and "not contend with others"(Ch. 22); and also means "does away with extremity, extravagance and excess"(Ch. 29).

This principle of anti-competition above, if put into practice by all the people, will surely give rise to a world of peace. But Lao Zi understands well that few people are capable of applying his principle to practice:"My words are very easy to understand, / And very easy to be put into practice, / Yet there should have been no one in the world / Who can understand them / Or can put them into practice... / Those who understand me are few; / Those who can follow my advice are even less."(Ch. 70) As a last resort, Lao Zi entices human beings to follow his principle by promising to give a high possibility of benefiting in one way or another. This is really a painstaking effort on the part of Lao Zi, a delicate strategy, a subtle inconsistency with the inaction theory preached by the Taoist. The idea of anticompetition later on develops into the

idea that peaceful coexistence is most valuable, forming a vital link in the psychological chain of traditional Chinese consciousness. Ignorance of this fact, therefore, is a clear indication of incomplete understanding of the Chinese spirit.

4.1.2 *The moderation of desires*

Man is born with three desires, the desire for food, the desire for sex, and the desire for power. The Tao of anti-competition calls for a repression of human desires, thus Lao Zi repeatedly advocates the theory of getting rid of desires. Lao Zi sees clearly that to get rid of desires completely is only an ideal without the hope of being fulfilled. Thus, as if attempting a compromise, Lao Zi suggests that one should "Discard selfishness and weaken desires."(Ch. 19) As a philosophical statement the idea of getting rid of desires is the most vulnerable. Since it is well known that man is born with natural desires, is it not against Nature itself if the desires are to be removed? To modern minds, the significance of life lies right in the justified satisfaction of human desires; therefore to root out human desires means to render man to a lower series of animal; consequently, man would be no longer entitled to the name of man but would become a lifeless object.

Then does Lao Zi really mean to get rid of human desire in its entirety? My answer is in the negative. Indeed, Lao Zi uses expressions like "desireless" (*Wuyu*), "without desires" or "getting rid of desires", but it would be too arbitrary to come to a conclusion that he is therefore an out-and-out asceticist. As is known, classical Chinese is characteristically vague in meaning. Hence we might do this Taoist philosopher injustice to take whatever he says at face value. Words like "without desires" and "getting rid of desires" are clearly intended to express a strong intention to suppress certain human desires. They are not, however, meant absolutely. For common people, "desireless" is used and understood in a general sense to mean moderation of desire, i. e. people should "Discard selfishness and weaken desires. / Discard culture and knowledge / and worries will disappear" (Ch. 19). The aim of moderation of desire is to help people "keep being simple in nature and mind" (Ch. 19), and to build up a society in which hypocrisy, trickery, suppression and exploitation are not allowed to come into effect. If Lao Zi really means to root out human desires, why does he appeal to construct a society in which "The people will have delicious food, / beautiful clothes, / comfortable living quarters, / cheerful customs" (Ch. 80)? Isn't that the best fulfillment of human desires?

Yet as a means to practice Qigong, the idea of getting rid of desires is indeed meant seriously. To enter into a Qigong state, a Qigong master needs to wash away all his distracting ideas which mostly come from desires. Thus getting rid of desires becomes a necessity for the successful Qigong meditation. Besides, for some people, Qigong especially calls for a suppression of sexual desires, because Taoists believe man's semen can generate Qi (air-like essence); a man who indulges in sexual pleasure can never get and store up enough Qi within his body.

The discussion above convinces us that the idea of "desireless" (*Wuyu*) should be interpreted in terms of its true connotation as 1) it is a moderation of desire for common people and 2) it means to get rid of desire as much as possible for those who are engaged in Qigong practice. The ignorance of the difference means the ignorance of the duality of Lao Zi's theory of *Wuyu* and thus often tempts scholars to conclude that Lao Zi is a pure asceticist.

4.1.3 *Keep being weak*

Another thought frequently repeated in *Lao Zi* is that the weak conquers the strong. "Everyone in the world knows / That the weak is more powerful than the strong, / That the supple is more rigid than the hard"(Ch. 78). Hence a realistic man should always take the side of the weak just as realistic states should resign themselves a lower position. "A large state should play the role of female, / Just like the lowest reaches of a river / Where all the other streams meet. / The female always conquers the male by motionlessness, / Because the motionless female always takes the lower position. / Hence the large state can annex the small one / by taking the lower position (being modest); / The small state can gain the trust of the large one by taking the lower position."(Ch. 61) By analogy the thought is further developed so that it becomes applicable in many aspects of life. "That is why the humble is the root of the noble, / And the high is based on the low. / That is why lords and kings call themselves 'the solitary', 'the few' and 'the unkind'. / Does not this take the humble as the root (of the noble)? / Does this not? Hence the highest honor does not need honoring. / It is better, therefore, to be a hard stone than a beautiful piece of jade"(Ch. 39). Lao Zi knows well: extremes meet; a clever man knows how to willingly stay on the degraded position though he is actually powerful: "Though knowing what is masculine, / You are ready to play the role of female / And content to be the lowest reaches of the world / ... Though knowing what is white, / You are ready to play the role of black... / Though knowing what is honor, / You are ready to play the role of the disgraced / And content to be a valley in the world..."(Ch. 28).

Dialectically speaking, this keeping-being-weak idea is subtly profound. On one hand, we know that it is almost equal to giving oneself up as hopeless, because one is bound to become more and more inactive if one sticks to it, and on the other, we understand that the conversion between the weak and strong is conditional, because the weak does not always conquer the strong. There is, so to speak, a period of transformation, during which the weak, after all, is weak, while the strong is strong. Lao Zi just ignores the time difference, stressing the weak unconditionally, thus he is often criticized for what is called "his limitations".

After all, Lao Zi's idea of keeping-being-weak is also often explained as compassionate understanding of the poor in a society where the strong overpowers the weak and severe struggle for existence is a common occurrence. So the idea of standing on the side of the weak is both historically and realistically significant for world peace and the well-being of mankind.

4.1.4 *Self-contentment with one's fate*

There is a shortcut to paradise or true happiness which one can easily find if he really understands Tao, that is, the idea of being content with one's fate: "He who knows contentment is rich"(Ch. 33); "Knowing contentment avoids disgrace; / Knowing when to stop avoids danger, / Thus one can be long in safety"(Ch. 44). What is happiness? Happiness, in my opinion, is nothing but a sense (a feeling) of self-satisfaction. There are two ways to gain that feeling: one way is to gain it by exposing one's body to external stimulations, say, satisfying one's desires for food, for sex, and for power, to one's heart's content; the other is to gain it through an (internal realization) introspection of the truth that happiness is only a consciousness of self-satisfaction, and thus happiness be gained by resorting to reason and illumination while reducing external stimulations to a minimum. Perhaps, the idea of being content with

one's fate is the greatest thought ever born of man's brain; it is hard to say who is in history the originator of the idea, but we do know, Lao Zi expresses it most precisely and concisely. This alone, I dare say, is enough to rank Lao Zi among the greatest thinkers of the world.

4.2 *Tao embodied in politics*

Just like his outlook upon life, Lao Zi's political idea is the live embodiment of his Tao, or we say, to a great degree, Lao Zi's politics is the very expression of his view of his life. Lao Zi's political ideas, which have been the target of attack from modern scholars, roughly fall into four categories: 1) inaction or non-interference; 2) disregarding the learned or talented; 3) simplifying people's minds; and 4) keeping the country small and the population sparse.

4.2.1 *Inaction or non-interference*

Politically the idea of inaction does not mean doing nothing at all but means doing things as naturally as possible, issuing orders as few as possible and interfering with people's life as little as possible: "Thus the sage behaves / Without taking active action, / Teaches without using words, / Let all things grow without interference"(Ch. 2); "Teaching without words, / The benefit of inaction, / are what few people in the world can perform and obtain."(Ch. 43); "Rule the state with peace and inaction"(Ch. 57); "Those who hold it by force will lose it. / Thus the sage never ruins anything because of his inaction; / He never loses anything"(Ch. 64). It is the very inaction that makes people do whatever they like: "When reaching the state of inaction, / one can succeed in everything. / To govern the world well, / one must take inaction as the principle. If one governs with too much action, / one is not a worthy governor" (Ch. 48). According to Lao Zi, the overeagerness of governing the people on the part of government leads to the result that "The more prohibitions there are in the world, / The poorer the people are"(Ch. 57). Therefore, the best policy is that of noninterference, or to use a Western term, laissez-faire. It is fitting for a government to exist only in name without taking trouble to enact any policies for the people. The more policies it makes, the more trouble it creates. Therefore, a government is not good because of so-called political achievements but because of its lack of political achievement: "The best ruler is unknown to his subjects; / Next comes the ruler loved and praised; / Next comes the ruler being feared; / Next comes the ruler disdained... / The best ruler is leisurely and carefree, / seldom issuing orders"(Ch. 17). Care about nothing and everything can be cared about well. This is a matter of following the law of Nature rather than following the law of Man. In this sense, Lao Zi can be regarded as the originator of ideas concerning market economy which is under the control of an invisible hand. It seems ideal, however, to attempt a compromise between the two: taking the former as the main approach and the latter as the supplement. After all, blindly carrying out the Taoist doctrine to the letter in world affairs can be also unrealistic and harmful to human beings.

4.2.2 *Disregarding the talented and learned*

The non-action policy being put into practice, the society does not need so many clever policy-makers. Thus there is no need to hold the talented and learned men in esteem: "Keep the people from contention by disregarding men of abilities"(Ch. 3). In the opinion of Lao Zi, the very cause of troubles of a

country stems from the wise and talented men who "are unruly / Because they are too clever. / Thus to govern a state by cleverness is bound to ruin the state; / Not to govern the state by cleverness / Is a blessing to the state"(Ch. 65).

In spite of the fact that even what seems to be the worst policy can be in one way or another put into good use, the availability of the Taoist inaction policy above is obviously challenged by another fact that human society is now highly advanced (civilized) with science and knowledge being the overwhelming impetus. We therefore see little chance for a policy of getting rid of desire and knowledge as well as talented men to be accepted, even by the most traditional citizens, let alone those in positions of power.

4.2.3 *Simplifying people's minds*

Along with the policy of the disregarding of men of abilities goes hand in hand the policy of simplifying people's minds, i. e. "That is why in governing the people / The sage simplifies their minds / but fills up their bellies; / weakens their wills, / but strengthens their bones. / By keeping the people from knowledge and desires, / He disables wise men / from taking any ill action. / Act in accordance with this principle of inaction / And the world will be kept in order everywhere"(Ch. 3); "Those ancient men of the profound Tao / Do not use Tao to enlighten the people / But use Tao to make them simple... / Thus to govern a state by cleverness / Is bound to ruin the state; / Not to govern the state by cleverness / Is a blessing to the state"(Ch. 65). With Lao Zi, the progress of science and technology brought forth by the steady accumulation of knowledge can not save mankind from suffering. Rather, knowledge often functions as a hindrance to the realization of the well-being of human beings, though it may not be a serious crime.

Some scholars deem Lao Zi's policy of simplifying people's minds as pure political trickery for the rulers. This I think is a misunderstanding. In fact Lao Zi totally opposes the existence of the ruling class by firmly maintaining an inaction policy whereby the rulers should not interfere in people's life and that laws and regulations should be abolished so that "people will naturally crave for peace..., will be naturally rectified;... will naturally become rich." (Ch. 57) In a sense, Lao Zi could be regarded as an anarchist. To say he is deliberately giving counsel for the rulers, therefore, is an obvious inconsistency with his Taoist system of politics. Moderns may think of the simplifying-minds policy as something bad while Lao Zi may just think of it otherwise. What is called "simplifying people's minds" in Lao Zi's mind means to help people become more honorably simple. It means to get rid of misleading knowledge, desires, hypocrisy, so that they can enjoy a true happiness in terms of Taoism. Lao Zi is strongly against suppression and exploitation: "While the court is corrupt, / The fields lie waste; / The granaries are empty; / There are persons who are still dressed gaudily, / Wearing ornamented swords, / Satiated with fine food and drink, / In possession of extravagant goods. / They can be called the chieftains of robbers. / What a phenomenon against Tao" (Ch. 53)! Again, in Chapter 75, Lao Zi attacks the rulers in a more direct manner: "The hunger on the part of the people / Is the result of exorbitant taxes on the part of the ruler; / Thus the people are hungry. / The unruliness on the part of the people / Is the result of the meddlesome actions on the part of the ruler; / Thus people are unruly. / Making light of life on the part of people / Is the result of setting too much store by life on the part of the ruler; / Thus the people make light of life. / Those who make light of their own life / Are wiser than those who overvalue their life." Lao Zi courageously directs his spearhead of criticism at lords and emperors who are, according to him, the true cause of hunger and social unrest.

Lao Zi warns: "When people are not afraid of death, / What is the point of threatening them with death"? (Ch.74) If the ruler is bent on the suppression of the people, sooner or later, the suppressor must be suppressed and the exploiter exploited. Whoever suppresses the people will inevitably be killed in a manner similar to chopping wood for the master carpenter: "There are few who can escape cutting their own hands / When they chop wood on behalf of the master carpenter"(Ch. 74).

4.2.4 *Keep the country small and population sparse*

A thinker who maintains an inaction policy of getting rid of knowledge and desires to make people live and develop in their own natural manner naturally tends to weaken or abrogate imperial power, in order to help people enjoy as much freedom as possible. Therefore I think Lao Zi is the earliest democratic and anti-war hero in Chinese history. This assertion is well-justified by his idea of keeping the country small and population sparse (Ch. 80) which is in a sharp contrast to the idea of expanding the territory of the country and increasing its population. Lao Zi sees clearly that the steady progress of human intelligence, the development of productive power, and the improvement of transportation is always accompanied with the frequent wars for the expansion of land; his remedy for such social evils is the following: "The state should be small, / The population should be sparse. / Tools, though of many kinds, / Should not be used. / Teach the people to fear death / And not to migrate to remote places. / Although they have ships and carts, / They will have no need to use them. / Although they are well armed with weapons, / They will have no place to make them effective. / Encourage the people to return to the condition under which the knotted rope was used to record things"(Ch. 80). He holds that, a smaller country with a sparse population makes it possible for its people to be self-reliant; the inconvenience of transportation reduces to the least degree chances to make contact with other peoples, hence avoids contamination from higher civilization; the ruler does not tend to interfere in people's life, the social order is not to be maintained by force, hence no taxes, no wars. People are honest and simple, enjoy to their heart's content delicious food, beautiful dresses, comfortable dwelling, delightful customs. To Lao Zi, the vast land with large population serves only as a means to further strengthen the authority of the ruler, yet it does people no good in satisfying their need for peace and the sense of self-contentment. Although the picture of small country and sparse population is just like an utopia in modern times, it is not totally impossible that in a new century the idea may again become a new hope for mankind.

4.3 *Lao Zi's outlook upon society and history*

Lao Zi's view of society in a historical perspective very much resembles his view of politics. The subjective purpose of advocating non-interference, disregarding men of abilities, simplifying people's minds, keeping the state small and rendering population sparse, is to make the human beings return to a primitive society of simplicity and equality in which people use knotted ropes to record things (Ch. 80); and the objective means to realize the purpose of anti-exploitation, anti-monarchy, anti-war as well as anti-knowledge, anti-science, and anti-civilization. Lao Zi's view of social and historical development comes from a philosopher's cool reasoning as well as from a Qigong master's bodily meditation. Exploitation, suppression, monarchy, wars and injustices all take root in innate human desires and postnatal knowledge. Thus a process of rooting out injustices must begin with the elimination of human desires, knowledge and

civilization. Needless to say, the view of this kind is hardly acceptable for modern minds, and is often criticized as Utopian, or retrogressive.

With the high development of human civilization, above all, the great expansion of modern science, the conflicts and contradictions in human societies are correspondingly intensified; the conflict between man as an individual, society and nature grows to a point that nothing can bridge the gap of conflict. "Return to Nature" was once a slogan echoed among some modern philosophers and sociologists. More and more scholars have realized that science is a two-edge sword that does mankind lots of good as well as lots of harm. Like everything else in the world, science develops its own logic and momentum with its tremendous advantages and disadvantages. What worries us is the question whether man is powerful and reasonable enough to make its advantages always overwhelmingly prevail over its disadvantages; if man has too many uncertainties about the question, a revaluation of Lao Zi's Taoist view of society and history is undoubtedly of functional significance for the modern world.

We are used to labeling Lao Zi's view of society and history as a backward theory, and from the angle of deve-lopment of civilization, we are probably right. But if it is viewed from an angle of true value-judgment, to say retrogression is bad surely is too hasty a conclusion that goes against Lao Zi's own Taoist logic. Observed from Lao Zi's anti-culture standpoint, "return to nature and simplicity" is indeed a regression, but the regression is deemed good for mankind, because the retrogression means a return to a society of peace and well-being. Taoistly speaking, "Cycling is the movement of Tao"; a thing can be both A and B. Thus retrogression is both a retreat and progress, i.e. a retreat from the age of hypocrisy to the age of simplicity, a progress from anti-Tao society to Tao-centered society. To view the primitive society of equality as the

most beautiful and most ideal means to regard the later civilized stages of social development as regressive. Even from the point of view of human physiological development, the same process happens: the development of the human brain is achieved at the price of the regression of human limbs and bodies; the growth and strengthening on the part of adulthood is accompanied by the steadily gradual loss of Yuan Qi (the natal energy) of childhood. Human bodies are two-way-oriented organic combinations: being both of the evolution and retrogression. If we do not understand this dialect pattern of thought typical of Taoism, we are apt to ignore Lao Zi's thought as backward and even, as some one terms, reactionary.

To me, the worry troubling modern minds is not the difficulty to make the choice of whether we should return to primitive society or not but the sudden awareness that human beings have long lost the abilities and power to go back to nature. Thus Lao Zi's view of society and history is only an ideal, a speculation of profound philosophical significance. It may, however, inspire modern people to restrain, if possible, social progress, hence to retard certain regressional processes in favour of the natural world.

Man's fate is fashioned by man's own choice. The views—usually useless— of philosophers serve only as a frame of reference for choice, we'd better let human beings make their own decisions, and, perhaps in terms of Taoism, this is exactly the attitude that conforms to Nature and Tao itself.

A Few Words about the Translation

Versions of *The Book of Lao Zi* are too many to be enumerated here. There is a belief that *Lao Zi* has been translated into any language available to the modern world. So great a philosophical work as *The Book of Tao and Teh* must

naturally call for a genuine sense of responsibility on the part of the translator; he is expected to be always very careful in rendering each line so that the original meaning and flavor can suffer less distortion. Most translators are apt to indulge themselves in interpreting rather than translating the original, so they occasionally impose their own ideas upon the author they translate. My means of avoiding such misreading and misinterpretation is to read as many of the annotated *The Book of Lao Tzu* in Chinese as possible. A list of them is annexed to the end of this book; often, when understanding of the original tends to be in too many directions, I carefully chose the one that is supposed to be preferred by modern scholars. It goes without saying that, I am not one who only cautiously follows in the wake of preceding scholars. I make my choice and have my say. There must be places where understanding of the original is different from other scholars' judgments. I have studied *Lao Zi* for more than 30 years and I am glad that I am now in a position to voice my own opinion by taking advantage of being a translator. If, I should say, there is something in my work that seems wide of the mark, I ask the reader to understand that, since so many versions have come into existence, one more version, my own, even if with some degree of deviation from the norm, is certainly tolerable.

Incidentally, the texts of *The Book of Tao and Teh* are all matched with Chinese phonetic symbols so that foreign readers can learn how to read the Chinese text. But I hasten to add that the pronunciation of them is not meant to be given according to the original sound of 2,000 years ago in ancient China but in most cases their contemporary and standard pronunciation. This is because 1) the old sound patterns are out of date even for modern Chinese readers; 2) since our offering the pronunciation is intended to help foreign readers learn modern Chinese, the old pronunciation is certainly quite unnecessary.

In trying to translate a philosophical masterpiece into English, I am made more than usually aware of my debt to earlier and contemporary scholars who have laboured in this field.   This debt is partially acknowledged in the bibliographical references annexed to the end of the book.   More personally， I am happy to express my thanks to colleagues and friends in UNESCO (Paris) and elsewhere whom I have consulted， and in particular to Professor Li Funing of Department of English，Peking University，for his brilliant guidance，to Dr. Tony Gallagher，an Australian expert，for his careful and adequate correction of my English introduction to the book. Also，in translating the book，I feel much in debt to Mr. Hu Shuangbao，editor-in-charge of the book (1995 edition)，Mr. Zhang Wending，deputy editor-in-chief of Peking University Press，Mr. Zhou Xueyi， director of foreign languages and literature section of Peking University Press，for their constructive suggestions. Finally，I'd like to express my sincere thanks to Zhao Hong，my wife，for her laborious proofreading of the manuscripts，without which，the present book would be much less than what it is.

First draft in
UNESCO Paris，France
September，1993

The first revision made at
Department of English
Peking University，
Beijing，100871，China
in May，1994

The second revision made at
Department of English
Peking University，
in August，2006

道 经

The Book of Tao

一 章

dào kě dào　fēi cháng dào
道 可 道 ， 非 常 道 ；

míng kě míng　fēi cháng míng
名 可 名 ， 非 常 名 。

wú　míng tiān dì zhī shǐ
無 ， 名 天 地 之 始 ；

yǒu　míng wàn wù zhī mǔ
有 ， 名 萬 物 之 母 。

gù cháng wú　yù yǐ guān qí miào
故 常 無 ， 欲 以 觀 其 妙 ，

cháng yǒu　yù yǐ guān qí jiào
常 有 ， 欲 以 觀 其 徼 。

cǐ liǎng zhě　tóng chū ér yì míng
此 兩 者 ， 同 出 而 異 名 。

tóng wèi zhī xuán
同 謂 之 玄 ，

xuán zhī yòu xuán
玄 之 又 玄 ，

zhòng miào zhī mén
衆 妙 之 門 。

Chapter 1

The Tao* that can be expressed in words

Is not the true and eternal Tao;

The name that can be uttered in words

Is not the true and eternal name.

The word Nothingness may be used

to designate the beginning of Heaven and Earth;

The word Existence (Being) may be used

to designate the mother of all things.

Hence one should gain an insight into the subtley

of Tao by observing Nothingness,

and should gain an insight into the beginning

of Tao by observing Existence (Being).

These two things, Nothingness and Existence,

Are of the same origin but different in name.

They are extremely profound in depth

Serving as the door of myriad secret beings.

* The Tao: (spelled as Dao in Chinese phonetic symbols) a philosophical term first used by Lao Tzu (Lao Zi); traditionally translated as Tao (thus Taoism), logos, way, path, road, etc.

二 章

tiān xià jiē zhī měi zhī wéi měi
天 下 皆 知 美 之 爲 美 ，

sī wù yǐ
斯 惡 矣 ；

jiē zhī shàn zhī wéi shàn
皆 知 善 之 爲 善

sī bù shàn yǐ
斯 不 善 矣 。

gù
故

yǒu wú xiāng shēng
有 無 相 生 ，

nán yì xiāng chéng
難 易 相 成 ，

cháng duǎn xiāng xíng
長 短 相 形 ，

gāo xià xiāng qīng
高 下 相 傾 ，

Chapter 2

The whole world knows the beautiful as beautiful,

Hence the existence of the ugly;

The whole world knows the good as good,

Hence the existence of the bad.

Therefore Existence and Nothingness

    beget each other;

Difficult and easy

    complement each other;

Long and short

    manifest themselves by comparison;

High and low are inclined

    as well as opposed to each other;

yīn shēng xiāng hè
音聲相和，
qián hòu xiāng suí
前後相隨。
shì yǐ shèng rén
是以聖人
chǔ wú wéi zhī shì
處無爲之事，
xíng bù yán zhī jiào
行不言之教；

wàn wù zuò ér fú shǐ
萬物作而弗始，
shēng ér fú yǒu
生而弗有，
wéi ér bù shì
爲而不恃，
gōng chéng ér fú jū
功成而弗居。
fū wéi fú jū
夫唯弗居，
shì yǐ bù qù
是以不去。

Musical sound and singing voice
      harmonize each other;
Front and back follow each other.
Thus the sage behaves
Without taking unnatural action,
Teaches without using words,
Lets all things grow without interference,
Gives them life without claiming to be their owner,
Benefits them
      without claiming to be their benefactor,
         succeeds without claiming credit.
Because he does not claim credit,
His credit is never lost.

三章

bù shàng xián   shǐ mín bù zhēng
不 尚 賢 ，使 民 不 争 ；

bù guì nán dé zhī huò
不 貴 難 得 之 貨 ，

shǐ mín bù wéi dào
使 民 不 爲 盗 ；

bù xiàn kě yù
不 見 可 欲 ，

shǐ mín xīn bù luàn
使 民 心 不 亂 。

shì yǐ shèng rén zhī zhì
是 以 聖 人 之 治 ，

xū qí xīn
虚 其 心 ，

shí qí fù
實 其 腹 ，

ruò qí zhì
弱 其 志 ，

qiáng qí gǔ
强 其 骨 ，

cháng shǐ mín wú zhī wú yù
常 使 民 無 知 無 欲 ；

shǐ fū zhì zhě bù gǎn wéi yě
使 夫 智 者 不 敢 爲 也 。

wéi wú wéi
爲 無 爲 ，

zé wú bù zhì
則 無 不 治 。

Chapter 3

Keep the people from contention
    by disregarding men of abilities；
Keep the people from theft
    by not valuing rare goods；
Keep the people from the disturbed
        state of mind
        by concealing what is desirable.
That is why in governing the people
The sage simplifies their minds
    fills up their stomachs，
    weakens their wills，
    and strengthens their bones.
By keeping the people
    from knowledge and desires，
He disables wise men
    from taking any ill action.
Act in accordance
    with this principle of inaction
And the world will be kept in order
    everywhere.

四章

dào chōng
道 冲 ，
  ér yòng zhī huò bù yíng
  而 用 之 或 不 盈 。
yuān xī
渊 兮 ，
  sì wàn wù zhī zōng
  似 万 物 之 宗 。
cuò qí ruì
挫 其 锐 ，
jiě qí fēn
解 其 纷 ；
hé qí guāng
和 其 光 ，
tóng qí chén
同 其 尘 ；
zhàn xī
湛 兮 ，
  sì huò cún
  似 或 存 。
wú bù zhī shuí zhī zǐ
吾 不 知 谁 之 子 ，
xiàng dì zhī xiān
象 帝 之 先 。

Chapter 4

Tao is invisibly empty,
But its use is extremely plentiful.
It is profound like the originator
    of all things.
It shows no sharpness,
    stays away from entanglements,
    glows with veiled radiance,
    mingles with dust.
It is formless and invisible,
    but indeed exists.
I do not know where it comes from
It seems to have appeared
    before the existence of God.

五 章

tiān dì bù rén
天 地 不 仁 ，

yǐ wàn wù wéi chú gǒu
以 萬 物 爲 芻 狗 ；

shèng rén bù rén
聖 人 不 仁 ，

yǐ bǎi xìng wéi chú gǒu
以 百 姓 爲 芻 狗 。

tiān dì zhī jiān
天 地 之 間 ，

qí yóu tuó yuè hū
其 猶 橐 籥 乎 ？

xū ér bù qū
虛 而 不 屈 ，

dòng ér yù chū
動 而 愈 出 。

duō yán shù qióng
多 言 數 窮 ，

bù rú shǒu zhōng
不 如 守 中 。

Chapter 5

Heaven and Earth are not merciful,
They treat all things as straw dogs*;
The sage is not merciful,
He treats the people as straw dogs.
Does not the space
    between heaven and earth
    function like a bellows?
It is empty but (the air in it)
    can never be exhausted;
The more air it expels,
    the more comes out.
That is why too many government decrees
    only result in more failures.
It is better, therefore, to hold fast
    to moderation and the void.

〇 一 三

* Straw dogs: a kind of offering used
by Chinese ancients for the purpose of
sacrifice ceremony, usually discarded
and trampled upon at the end of the
ceremony.

六 章

gǔ shén bù sǐ
谷神不死，
　　shì wèi xuán pìn
　　是谓玄牝。
xuán pìn zhī mén
玄牝之门，
　　shì wèi tiān dì gēn
　　是谓天地根。
mián mián ruò cún
绵绵若存，
yòng zhī bù qín
用之不勤。

Chapter 6

Tao never dies;

It is a deep womb.

And the opening of the womb

Is called the root of heaven and earth.

It exists for ever,

And its use can never be exhausted.

七 章

tiān cháng dì jiǔ
天 长 地 久。

tiān dì suǒ yǐ néng cháng qiě jiǔ zhě
天 地 所 以 能 长 且 久 者，

yǐ qí bù zì shēng
以 其 不 自 生，

gù néng cháng shēng
故 能 长 生。

shì yǐ shèng rén
是 以 圣 人

hòu qí shēn ér shēn xiān
後 其 身 而 身 先，

wài qí shēn ér shēn cún
外 其 身 而 身 存。

fēi yǐ qí wú sī yé
非 以 其 無 私 邪？

gù néng chéng qí sī
故 能 成 其 私。

Chapter 7

Heaven and Earth exist for ever.

This eternal existence is justified by the fact

That they do not exist for themselves.

Thus they enjoy an eternal life.

The sage similarly puts himself behind others,

Yet it turns out that he comes before others；

He completely disregards his own existence,

And yet it turns out that his existence is preserved.

八 章

shàng shàn ruò shuǐ
上 善 若 水 。

shuǐ shàn lì wàn wù ér bù zhēng
水 善 利 萬 物 而 不 争 ，

chǔ zhòng rén zhī suǒ wù
處 衆 人 之 所 惡 ，

gù jī yú dào
故 幾 於 道 。

jū shàn dì
居 善 地 ，

xīn shàn yuān
心 善 淵 ，

yǔ shàn rén
与 善 仁 ，

yán shàn xìn
言 善 信 ，

zhèng shàn zhì
政 善 治 ，

shì shàn néng
事 善 能 ，

dòng shàn shí
動 善 時 。

fū wéi bù zhēng
夫 唯 不 争 ，

gù wú yóu
故 無 尤 。

Chapter 8

The perfect goodness is like water.

Water approaches all things

instead of contending with them.

It prefers to dwell where no one

would like to stay；

Hence it comes close to Tao.

A man of perfect goodness

chooses a low place to dwell as water，

He has a heart as deep as water，

He offers friendship as tender as water，

He speaks as sincerely as water，

He rules a state as orderly as water，

He does a thing as properly as water，

He takes action as timely as water.

Like water, he never contends with others，

So he never commits a mistake.

九 章

chí ér yíng zhī
持 而 盈 之 ，

bù rú qí yǐ
不 如 其 已 ；

zhuī ér ruì zhī
揣 而 锐 之 ，

bù kě cháng bǎo
不 可 长 保 。

jīn yù mǎn táng
金 玉 满 堂 ，

mò zhī néng shǒu
莫 之 能 守 。

fù guì ér jiāo
富 贵 而 骄 ，

zì yí qí jiù
自 遗 其 咎 。

gōng chéng shēn tuì
功 成 身 退 ，

tiān zhī dào yě
天 之 道 也 。 *

* 郭店楚简：攻(功)述身退,天之道也。

Chapter 9

One should stop in due time
Rather than fill it to the brim.
When a point is whittled too sharp,
Its sharpness cannot remain long.
When a hall is full of gold and jade,
Nobody can keep them long;
When a man of wealth and rank is arrogant,
He is looking for a calamity upon himself;
When one succeeds and subsequently retires,*
He follows the true way of Heaven.

---

* Guodian Chu Slips: It is the true way of
heaven for one to retire/when his achievement
is known and recorded.

十 章

zǎi yíng pò bào yī
载营魄抱一，

néng wú lí hū
能无离乎？

zhuān qì zhì róu
专气致柔，

néng rú yīng ér hū
能如婴儿乎？

dí chú xuán lǎn
涤除玄览，

néng wú cī hū
能无疵乎？

ài mín zhì guó
爱民治国，

néng wú wéi hū
能无为乎？

tiān mén kāi hé
天门开阖，

néng wéi cí hū
能为雌乎？

Chapter 10

Body and soul are one,

But can they avoid separation?

Though concentrating on breathing exercises

    (Qigong) to be supple,

Can you finally become as supple as a baby?

Though getting rid of your distracting thoughts

    for a deeper meditation,

Can you be devoid of blemish?

If you are to love the people and govern a state,

Can you avoid taking ill action?

When the door of Heaven opens or closes,*

Can you remain inactive as a female?

---

* The door of heaven(天門); The interpretations for 天門 are many. They are 1) the nose; 2)
the source of peace as well as troubles; 3) the law of nature; 4) the opening where
consciousness enters and gets out; 5) organs of senses.

    According to my experience of Qigong exercies, it is the Baihui(百会) point on top
of the head, which functions as a door linking up nature and body, thus the fifth
interpretation is more acceptable.

míng bái sì dá
明 白 四 達，

néng wú zhì hū
能 無 知 乎？

shēng zhī xù zhī
生 之 畜 之，

shēng ér bù yǒu
生 而 不 有，

wéi ér bù shì
爲 而 不 恃，

zhǎng ér bù zǎi
長 而 不 宰，

shì wèi xuán dé
是 謂 玄 德。

When your power of perception

      penetrates every corner,

Are you capable of knowing nothing?

Giving all things life and propagation

Without claiming to be their owner,

Benefiting them without claiming

      to be their benefactor,

And being their head without ruling them,

All these are called

      the most intrinsic Teh (virtue).

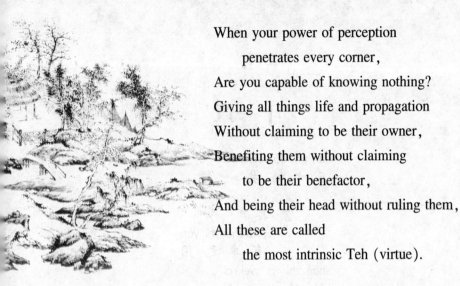

十一章

sān shí fú gǒng yī gǔ
三十辐共一毂，

dāng qí wú
当其无，

yǒu chē zhī yòng
有车之用。

shān zhí yǐ wéi qì
埏埴以为器，

dāng qí wú
当其无，

yǒu qì zhī yòng
有器之用。

záo hù yǒu yǐ wéi shì
凿户牖以为室，

dāng qí wú
当其无，

yǒu shì zhī yòng
有室之用。

gù yǒu zhī yǐ wéi lì
故有之以为利，

wú zhī yǐ wéi yòng
无之以为用。

Chapter 11

Thirty spokes share one hub.

It is just the space (the Nothingness)

    between them

That makes a cart function as a cart.

Knead clay to make a vessel

And you find within it the space

That makes a vessel as a vessel.

Within a house built with doors and windows

You will find the space

That makes a house function as a house.

Hence the substance (Being)

    can provide a condition

Under which usefulness is found,

But the Nothingness (space)

    is the usefulness itself.

十二章

wǔ sè lìng rén mù máng
五色令人目盲；

wǔ yīn lìng rén ěr lóng
五音令人耳聋；

wǔ wèi lìng rén kǒu shuǎng
五味令人口爽；

chí chěng tián liè lìng rén xīn fā kuáng
驰骋畋猎令人心发狂；

nán dé zhī huò lìng rén xíng fáng
难得之货令人行妨。

shì yǐ
是以

shèng rén wèi fù bù wèi mù
圣人为腹不为目。

gù qù bǐ qǔ cǐ
故去彼取此。

Chapter 12

The five colours* make man blind;
The five sounds** make man deaf;
The five tastes*** make man
    lose his sense of taste;
Riding and hunting make man
    wild with excitement;
Rare goods goad man into stealing;
Thus the sage does not satisfy
    his eyes with colours but
Satisfies his belly with enough food.
He discards the former and takes the latter.

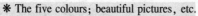

* The five colours; beautiful pictures, etc.
** The five sounds; beautiful music.
*** The five tastes; delicious food.

十三章

chǒng rǔ ruò jīng
寵　辱　若　驚，*

guì dà huàn ruò shēn
貴　大　患　若　身。

hé wèi chǒng rǔ ruò jīng
何　謂　寵　辱　若　驚？

chǒng wéi xià
寵　爲　下，

dé zhī ruò jīng
得　之　若　驚，

shī zhī ruò jīng
失　之　若　驚，

shì wèi chǒng rǔ ruò jīng
是　謂　寵　辱　若　驚。

hé wèi guì dà huàn ruò shēn
何　謂　貴　大　患　若　身？

wú suǒ yǐ yǒu dà huàn zhě
吾　所　以　有　大　患　者，

wèi wú yǒu shēn
爲　吾　有　身；

jí wú wú shēn
及　吾　無　身，

wú yǒu hé huàn
吾　有　何　患？

gù
故

guì yǐ shēn wèi tiān xià
貴　以　身　爲　天　下，

ruò kě jì tiān xià
若　可　寄　天　下；

ài yǐ shēn wèi tiān xià
愛　以　身　爲　天　下，

ruò kě tuō tiān xià
若　可　託　天　下。

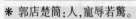

＊ 郭店楚簡：人，寵辱若驚。

Chapter 13

Honor and disgrace are both startling.*
It is like cherishing great trouble (vanity)
    as one's life and body.
What is meant by saying
    that honor and disgrace are startling?
Honor itself, though mean,
    gives pleasant surprise
    to those who obtain it
As well as startles them when they lose it.
What is meant by saying
    that it is like cherishing great trouble
    as one's life and body?
Because my life and body
    is the very source of great trouble.
If I have no body and life,
What trouble can I suffer?
Thus he who can value the empire
    as he values his own life and body
Can be entrusted with the care of the empire.
Thus he who can cherish the empire
    as he cherishes his own life and body
Can be entrusted with the care of the empire.

＊ Guodian Chu Slips: Oh, man, it is equally startling to be honored or dishonored.

十四章

shì zhī bù jiàn　　míng yuē yí
視之不見，名曰夷，

tīng zhī bù wén　　míng yuē xī
聽之不聞，名曰希，

bó zhī bù dé　　míng yuē wēi
搏之不得，名曰微。

cǐ sān zhě bù kě zhì jié
此三者不可致詰，

gù hùn ér wéi yī
故混而爲一。

qí shàng bù jiǎo
其上不皦，

qí xià bù mèi
其下不昧，

shéng shéng bù kě míng
繩　繩不可名，

fù guī yú wú wù
復歸於無物。

Chapter 14

What cannot be seen is called

"Yi" (without colour);

What cannot be heard is called

"Xi"(without sound);

What cannot be touched is called

"Wei"(without shape);

These three things

can be in no way defined,

So they are combined into one.

Above it there is no light;

Below it there is no darkness;

So vague as to defy any description.

It is categorized as Nothingness,

shì wèi wú zhuàng zhī zhuàng
是謂無狀之狀，

wú wù zhī xiàng
無物之象，

shì wèi hū huǎng
是謂惚恍。

yíng zhī bù jiàn qí shǒu
迎之不見其首；

suí zhī bù jiàn qí hòu
隨之不見其後。

zhí gǔ zhī dào yǐ yù jīn zhī yǒu
執古之道以御今之有，

néng zhī gǔ shǐ
能知古始，

shì wèi dào jì
是謂道紀。

And is called the shape without shape
    as well as the image without substance.
It is hence named as "huhuang"
    (vague and dimly visible).
Facing it, you cannot see its front;
Following it, you cannot see its back.
To control the present Being (substance)
    by employing the Tao of ancient time,
One knows the beginning of the universe.
And this is called the law of Tao.

十五章

gǔ zhī shàn wéi shì zhě
古 之 善 爲 士 者，

wēi miào xuán tōng
微 妙 玄 通，

shēn bù kě shí
深 不 可 識。

fú wéi bù kě shí
夫 惟 不 可 識，

gù qiǎng wéi zhī róng
故 强 爲 之 容：＊

yù xī ruò dōng shè chuān
豫 兮，若 冬 涉 川，

yóu xī ruò wèi sì lín
猶 兮，若 畏 四 鄰，

yǎn xī qí ruò róng
俨 兮，其 若 容，

huàn xī ruò bīng zhī jiāng shì
涣 兮，若 冰 之 將 釋，

dūn xī qí ruò pǔ
敦 兮，其 若 樸，

＊郭店楚簡：長古之善為士者，
　　必隱弱玄達，深不可志(識)，
　　是以為之頌(容)；

Chapter 15

Those ancients who were well versed
    in Tao
Were so subtle, mysterious and profound
As to escape understanding.
As they were beyond comprehension,
The description of them is surely perfunctory:＊
    careful as if fording a river barefoot in winter;
    vigilant and hesitant as if in fear
    of the attacks from neighbours;
    formal as if they were guests;
    polishedly flowing like melting ice;
    simple and natural like the uncarved block;

＊ Guodian Chu Slips: Those primordial ancients who were well
versed in Tao / must be so recluse, effeminate, mysterious
and profound / that they escape understanding, / and that
therefore I need to give a description of them:

kuàng xī   qí ruò gǔ
旷 兮 ，其 若 谷 ，

hùn xī   qí ruò zhuó
混 兮 ，其 若 浊 ，

dàn xī   qí ruò hǎi
澹 兮 ，其 若 海 ，

liáo xī   ruò wú zhǐ
飂 兮 ，若 無 止 。

shú néng zhuó yǐ zhǐ
孰 能 濁 以 止 ？

jìng zhī xú qīng
静 之 徐 清 。

shú néng ān yǐ jiǔ
孰 能 安 以 久 ？

dòng zhī xú shēng
動 之 徐 生 。

bǎo cǐ dào zhě bù yù yíng
保 此 道 者 不 欲 盈 。

fú wéi bù yíng
夫 惟 不 盈 ，

gù néng bì ér xīn chéng
故 能 蔽 而 新 成 。

vacant and deep like a valley;

turbid like muddy water.

quiet and calm like the great sea;

drifting as if they would never stop.

Who can end the muddiness

And make the muddy settle

and gradually become clear?

Who can be at rest and yet,

stirring, slowly come to life?

He who is in possession of this Tao

will not seek completeness.

Just because he will not seek completeness,

He can be both old and new.

十六章

zhì xū jí shǒu jìng dǔ
致虚極，守静篤。*

wàn wù bìng zuò
萬物並作，

wú yǐ guān fù
吾以觀復。

fú wù yún yún
夫物芸芸，

gè fù guī qí gēn
各復歸其根。

guī gēn yuē jìng
歸根曰静，

shì yuē fù mìng
是曰復命。

fù mìng yuē cháng
復命曰常，

zhī cháng yuē míng
知常曰明。

＊ 郭店楚簡：至虚，恒也；獸(守)中，篤也。
辜按：亦有學者認為"獸(守)中"即守中庸之
道，云云。

Chapter 16

I try my best to be in an extreme
     emptiness of mind；

I try to keep myself in a state of stillness.*

From the vigorous growth of all things

I perceive the way they move
     in endless cycles.

All things，full of vitality，

Finally return to their own roots.

Returning to roots means stillness，

Also means a return to destiny.

A return to destiny is known
     as the law of eternity.

To understand the law is known
     as enlightening.

＊ Guodian Chu Slips: Persistently stay in an extreme emptiness of mind; / earnestly concentrate
oneself on the central part of the body (Dantian).

Translator's note: Some scholars understand 歌(守)中 as observing the doctrine of mean.

bù zhī cháng　wàng zuò xiōng
不知常，妄作凶。

zhī cháng róng
知常容，

róng nǎi gōng
容乃公，

gōng nǎi quán
公乃全，

quán nǎi tiān
全乃天，

tiān nǎi dào
天乃道，

dào nǎi jiǔ
道乃久，

mò shēn bù dài
殁身不殆。

He who is ignorant of the law,

　　if acting rashly,

Will be in great trouble.

But he who knows the law is tolerant,

And the tolerance leads to impartiality;

Impartiality to thoroughness;

Thoroughness to nature;

Nature to Tao;

Tao to eternity.

Thus he will not be endangered all his life.

十七章

tài shàng xià zhī yǒu zhī
太 上 ，下 知 有 之 ，

qí cì qīn ér yù zhī
其 次 ，亲 而 誉 之 ；

qí cì wèi zhī
其 次 ，畏 之 ；

qí cì wǔ zhī
其 次 ，侮 之 ；

xìn bù zú yān
信 不 足 焉 ，

yǒu bù xìn yān
有 不 信 焉 ！

yōu xī qí guì yán
悠 兮 ，其 贵 言 ，

gōng chéng shì suì
功 成 事 遂 ，

bǎi xìng jiē wèi wǒ zì rán
百 姓 皆 谓 "我 自 然"。

Chapter 17

The best ruler is vaguely know to his subjects;
Next comes the ruler loved and praised;
Next comes the ruler being feared;
Next comes the ruler disdained.
The lack of faith on the part of the ruler
Leads to the lack of the people's confidence in him.
The best ruler is leisurely and carefree,
    seldom issuing orders.
When the state affairs are properly dealt with,
The people all say,
"It should have happened to us like this."

十八章

dà dào fèi
大 道 廢 ，

　　yǒu rén yì
　　有 仁 義 。

zhì huì chū
智 慧 出 ，

　　yǒu dà wěi
　　有 大 偽 。

liù qīn bù hé
六 親 不 和 ，

　　yǒu xiào cí
　　有 孝 慈 。

guó jiā hūn luàn
國 家 昏 亂 ，

　　yǒu zhōng chén
　　有 忠 臣 。

Chapter 18

The advocating of benevolence and rectitude
Stems from the disuse of the great Tao.
The great hypocrisy
Follows the emergence of cleverness
    and wisdom.
Filiality and benevolence come
Along with the family feud.
The loyal subjects show themselves
When the state is in great disorder.

十九章

jué shèng qì zhì
絶聖棄智，*

mín lì bǎi bèi
民利百倍；

jué rén qì yì
絶仁棄義，

mín fù xiào cí
民復孝慈；**

jué qiǎo qì lì
絶巧棄利，

＊ 郭店楚簡：絕智棄辨。

＊＊ 郭店楚簡：絕偽棄慮，民複季(稚)子。

辜按：此为郭店楚简本《老子》中含义更动最大的语句。通行本中的"絕聖弃智"和"絕仁棄義"在郭店楚简本中分别是"絕智棄辨"和"絕偽棄慮"。若干学者颇为兴奋，认为由此可得出定论：老子并不真正反对"仁"这个观念。他们并且推论，"絕聖弃智"和"絕仁棄義"这种观念一定是后来的庄子及其门徒强加于老子文本的。既然郭店墓主同时收藏阅读老子的文本和儒家文本，并且老子并不反对"仁"，学者们都乐于认为儒道两家当时并不势同水火，至少并未有所冲突。对此，我有自己的看法，另文，不赘。

Chapter 19

Discard cleverness and wisdom*
And the people will benefit themselves
    a hundredfold;
Discard benevolence and rectitude
And the people will again become

filial and loyal;**
Discard ingenuity and profit

---

  * Guodian Chu Slips: Discard wisdom and eloquence.
* * Guodian Chu Slips: Discard hypocrisy and misgivings, / And the people will restore to
    being like babies.
Translator's note: These few lines are supposed to be the most important changes in the text of
Lao Zi where 絕聖弃智 and 絕仁棄義 are respectively replaced by 絕智棄辨 and 絕偽棄慮.
Some scholars thus vehemently conclude that this is the firm proof that Lao Zi was not really
against Benevolence (*Ren*仁) and that the ideas of discarding benevolence and rectitude (绝仁弃
义) and discarding sages and wisdom (绝圣弃智) must have been just the ideas of Zhuang Zi
and his disciples who later on imposed the ideas on the Taoist texts. Since Lao Zi's texts were
read and collected together with Confucian texts and since Lao Zi is believed not to be against
Ren, some Chinese scholars feel ready to suggest that Taoism and Confucianism were not hostile
to each other, at least they did not go into conflict in their time. I wrote an article to voice my
different opinion of the argument to be published recently in a journal.

dào zéi wú yǒu
盗賊無有。

cǐ sān zhě yǐ wéi wén bù zú
此三者以爲文不足，

gù lìng yǒu suǒ shǔ
故令有所屬；

jiàn sù bào pǔ
見素抱樸，

shǎo sī guǎ yù
少私寡欲。

jué xué wú yōu
絶學無憂。

And theft will no longer exist.

It is not enough to have these points

as governing principles,

So the people must be made subject

to the following：

Keep being simple in nature and mind,

Discard selfishness and weaken desires.

Discard cultural knowledge

and worries will disappear.

二十章

wéi zhī yǔ ē
唯之与阿，

xiāng qù jǐ hé
　相去幾何？

shàn zhī yǔ è
善之与惡，

xiāng qù ruò hé
　相去若何？

rén zhī suǒ wèi　　bù kě bù wèi
人之所畏，不可不畏，

huāng xī　　qí wèi yāng zāi
荒兮，其未央哉！

zhòng rén xī　xī
眾人熙熙，

rú xiǎng tài láo
如享太牢，

rú chūn dēng tái
如春登臺。

wǒ dú bó xī　　qí wèi zhào
我獨泊兮，其未兆，

dùn dùn xī　　rú yīng ér zhī wèi hái
沌沌兮，如嬰兒之未孩，

Chapter 20

How much difference is seen
Between Yes and No?
How much dispairity is shown
Betwccn good and cvil?
If what other people fear
One must fear,
Then what a sea of fears—so vast and endless!
The multitude are jubilant
As if enjoying a magnificent feast
Or ascending a terrace to command a view
　　of spring scene.
While I, alone and inactive, remain
　　aloof and indifferent,
Like a baby that has not yet learned to smile;

○五三

lěi lěi xī   ruò wú suǒ guī
儽儽兮，若無所歸！

zhòng rén jiē yǒu yú
眾人皆有餘，

ér wǒ dú ruò kuì
而我獨若遺。

wǒ yú rén zhī xīn yě zāi
我愚人之心也哉！

sú rén zhāo zhāo
俗人昭昭，

wǒ dú hūn hūn
我獨昏昏。

sú rén chá chá
俗人察察，

wǒ dú mèn mèn
我獨悶悶。

zhòng rén jiē yǒu yǐ
眾人皆有以，

ér wǒ dú wán sì bǐ
而我獨頑似鄙。

wǒ dú yì yú rén
我獨異於人，

ér guì shí mǔ
而貴食母。

I am tired, like a homeless wanderer.

The multitude all have more than enough,

While I, alone, seem to have nothing.

I am one, indeed, with a heart of a fool.

Vulgar people all look sober and complacent,

While I alone seem muddleheaded.

The multitude all appear clever and capable,

While I alone seem slow-witted and clumsy.

I am indeed different from them all

Because I take the greatest interest in obtaining Tao.

二十一章

kǒng dé zhī róng
孔 德 之 容 ，

wéi dào shì cóng
惟 道 是 從 。

dào zhī wéi wù
道 之 爲 物 ，

wéi huǎng wéi hū
惟 恍 惟 惚 。

hū xī huǎng xī
惚 兮 恍 兮 ，

qí zhōng yǒu xiàng
其 中 有 象 ；

huǎng xī hū xī
恍 兮 惚 兮 ，

qí zhōng yǒu wù
其 中 有 物 ；

yǎo xī míng xī
窈 兮 冥 兮 ，

qí zhōng yǒu jīng
其 中 有 精 ，

qí jīng shèn zhēn
其 精 甚 真 ，

qí zhōng yǒu xìn
其 中 有 信 。

zì gǔ jí jīn
自 古 及 今 ，

qí míng bù qù
其 名 不 去 ，

yǐ yuè zhòng fǔ
以 閱 衆 甫 。

wú hé yǐ zhī zhòng fǔ zhī zhuàng zāi
吾 何 以 知 衆 甫 之 狀 哉 ？

yǐ cǐ
以 此 。

Chapter 21

The forms of the great Teh (virtue)

Exclusively depend on Tao.

Tao as a thing

Is vague and indefinite.

Vague and indefinite,

It presents images;

Indefinite and vague,

It embodies substance.

Distant and dark,

It embraces semen-like essence.

The essence is a genuine existence

That can be tested as true.

From ancient times to now,

Its name has always been accepted,

And with which, the beginning of all things
  can be surveyed.

How do I know the initial state
  of all things?

By means of Tao.

二十二章

qū zé quán
曲则全，

wǎng zé zhí
枉则直，

wā zé yíng
窪则盈，

bì zé xīn
弊则新，

shǎo zé dé
少则得，

duō zé huò
多则惑。

shì yǐ shèng rén bào yī wéi tiān xià shì
是以圣人抱一为天下式。

bù zì xiàn gù míng
不自见，故明；

bù zì shì gù zhāng
不自是，故彰；

bù zì fá gù yǒu gōng
不自伐，故有功；

Chapter 22

Bow down and you are preserved;

Bend and you can be straight;

Hollow, then new;

Worn, then full;

Seek a little and you get a lot;

Thus the sage adheres to this One principle (Tao)

And regards it as the pattern of all things.

Show off yourself not and you become conspicuous;

Regard yourself not as infallible

    and you become illustrious;

Brag about yourself not

    and you gain achievement;

bù zì jīn　gù cháng
不自矜，故长。

fú wéi bù zhēng
夫惟不争，

　　gù tiān xià mò néng yǔ zhī zhēng
　　故天下莫能与之争。

gǔ zhī suǒ wèi　qū zé quán　zhě
古之所谓"曲则全"者，

qǐ xū yán zāi
岂虚言哉？

chéng quán ér guī zhī
诚全而归之。

Boast of yourself not
and you become a head.
One does not contend with others,
So nobody in the world can win him
in contention.
The ancients' saying "Bow down
and you are preserved"
Is surely not an empty saying,
Which can be really proved effective.

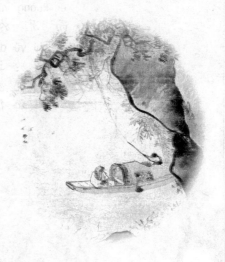

二十三章

xī yán zì rán
希 言 自 然 。

gù piāo fēng bù zhōng zhāo
故 飘 風 不 終 朝 ，

zhòu yǔ bù zhōng rì
驟 雨 不 終 日 。

shú wéi cǐ zhě
孰 爲 此 者 ？

tiān dì
天 地 。

tiān dì shàng bù néng jiǔ
天 地 尚 不 能 久 ，

ér kuàng yú rén hū
而 况 於 人 乎 ？

gù cóng shì yú dào zhě tóng yú dào
故 從 事 於 道 者 同 於 道 ，

dé zhě tóng yú dé
德 者 同 於 德 ，

Chapter 23

To be taciturn is in accordance with nature,

So much as a wanton wind

Does not last all morning,

And a sudden rain does not last all day.

Who makes it?

Heaven and Earth.

If Heaven and Earth cannot make it last long,

How can man?

So a man of Tao conforms to Tao;

A man of Teh to Teh;

shī zhě tóng yú shī
失 者 同 於 失 。

tóng yú dào zhě
同 於 道 者 ，

dào yì lè dé zhī
道 亦 樂 得 之 ；

tóng yú dé zhě
同 於 德 者 ，

dé yì lè dé zhī
德 亦 樂 得 之 ；

tóng yú shī zhě
同 於 失 者 ，

shī yì lè dé zhī
失 亦 乐 得 之 。

xìn bù zú yān
信 不 足 焉 ，

yǒu bù xìn yān
有 不 信 焉 ！

道 德 经

Λ man of having neither to the principle

of losing both above.

He who conforms to Tao

is readily received by Tao；

He who conforms to Teh

is readily received by Teh；

He who conforms to the principle

of losing both above

is readily discarded by the principle of loss.

The lack of faith on the part of the ruler

Leads to the lack of the people's confidence in him.

〇六五

二十四章

qǐ zhě bù lì
企者不立；

kuà zhě bù xíng
跨者不行；

zì xiàn zhě bù míng
自見者不明；

zì shì zhě bù zhāng
自是者不彰；

zì fá zhě wú gōng
自伐者無功；

zì jīn zhě bù zhǎng
自矜者不長。

qí zài dào yě
其在道也，

yuē yú shí zhuì xíng
曰餘食贅行，

wù huò wù zhī
物或惡之，

gù yǒu dào zhě bù chǔ
故有道者不處。

Chapter 24

He who stands on tiptoes
    cannot stand well;
He who walks with great strides
    cannot walk well;
He who shows off himself
    cannot become conspicuous;
He who regards himself infallible
    cannot become illustrious;
He who brags about himself
    cannot gain achievement;
He who boasts of himself
    cannot become a head.
From the point of view of Tao,
These behaviours are like leftover food
    and superfluous excrescence,
So disgusting that a man of Tao
Never behaves like that.

二十五章

yǒu wù hùn chéng
有物混成,

xiān tiān dì shēng
先天地生。

jì xī liáo xī
寂兮寥兮,

dú lì ér bù gǎi
獨立而不改,*

zhōu xíng ér bù dài
周行而不殆,

kě yǐ wéi tiān dì mǔ
可以爲天地母。

wú bù zhī qí míng
吾不知其名,

qiáng zì zhī yuē dào
强字之曰道,

qiáng wéi zhī míng yuē dà
强爲之名曰大。

dà yuē shì
大曰逝,

＊ 郭店楚簡:磷(奪)穆、蜀(獨)立、不亥(垓)

Chapter 25

There is a thing integratedly formed

And born earlier than Heaven and Earth.

Silent and empty,

It relies on nothing,＊

Moving around for ever.

We may regard it as the mother of all things.

I do not know its name,

So I name it as Tao,

And further name it as Great.

Great is moving forward

    without stopping,

＊ Guodian Chu Slips: it is solemn, self-independent and bound-
less

shì yuē yuǎn
逝曰遠，

yuǎn yuē fǎn
遠曰反。

gù dào dà
故道大，

tiān dà
天大，

dì dà
地大，

rén yì dà
人亦大。

yù zhōng yǒu sì dà
域中有四大，

ér rén jū qí yī yān
而人居其一焉。

rén fǎ dì
人法地，

dì fǎ tiān
地法天，

tiān fǎ dào
天法道，

dào fǎ zì rán
道法自然。

Extending to the remotest distance,
And then returning to where it was.
That is why I say
Tao is Great;
Heaven is Great;
Earth is Great;
And man is also Great.
There are four things that are Great,
Of them man is one.
Man takes Earth as his model;
Earth takes Heaven as its model;
Heaven takes Tao as its model;
Tao takes what is natural as its model.

二十六章

zhòng wéi qīng gēn
重　爲　輕　根，

jìng wéi zào jūn
静　爲　躁　君。

shì yǐ
是以

shèng rén zhōng rì xíng
聖人　終　日　行

bù lí zī zhòng
不　離　輜　重，

suī yǒu róng guān
雖　有　榮　觀，

yān chǔ chāo rán
燕　處　超　然。

nài hé wàn shèng zhī zhǔ
奈何　萬　乘　之　主

ér yǐ shēn qīng tiān xià
而以　身　輕　天　下？

qīng zé shī gēn
輕　則　失　根，

zào zé shī jūn
躁　則　失　君。

Chapter 26

Heaviness is the root of lightness.

Tranquillity is the lord of movement.

That is why the sage is always accompanied

    by his heavily laden cart

When he travels all day long.

Though he has a luxurious life to enjoy,

He never indulges himself in it.

Why should a ruler of ten thousand chariots

Take reckless action to govern the empire?

Lightness leads to the loss of the root;

Restlessness leads to the loss of the lord.

二十七章

shàn xíng　　wú zhé jì
善 行 , 無 轍 迹 ;

shàn yán　　wú xiá zhé
善 言 , 無 瑕 讁 ;

shàn shǔ　　bù yòng chóu cè
善 數 , 不 用 籌 策 ;

shàn bì　　wú guān jiàn ér bù kě kāi
善 閉 , 無 關 楗 而 不 可 開 ;

shàn jié　　wú shéng yuē ér bù kě jiě
善 結 , 無 繩 約 而 不 可 解 。

shì yǐ
是 以

shèng rén cháng shàn jiù rén
聖 人 常 善 救 人 ,

gù wú qì rén
故 無 棄 人 ;

cháng shàn jiù wù
常 善 救 物 ,

Chapter 27

He who is good at walking
    leaves no traces;
He who is good at speaking
    leaves no slips；
He who is good at counting
    uses no counting tools；
He who is good at shutting
    renders all efforts of opening
    in vain though he uses no bolts.
He who is good at tying
    renders all efforts of untying
    in vain though he uses no ropes；
That is why the sage
Is always good at saving people

gù wú qì wù
故 無 棄 物 。

shì wèi xí míng
是 謂 襲 明 。

gù
故

shàn rén zhě bù shàn rén zhī shī
善 人 者 不 善 人 之 師 ，

bù shàn rén zhě shàn rén zhī zī
不 善 人 者 善 人 之 資 。

bù guì qí shī
不 貴 其 師 ，

bù ài qí zī
不 愛 其 資 ，

suī zhì dà mí
雖 智 大 迷 。

shì wèi yào miào
是 謂 要 妙 。

And abandoning no one；

That is why the sage

  is always good at saving things

  and abandoning nothing.

This is called the intrinsic wisdom.

Thus the good man

  is the bad man's teacher；

The bad man is the material ′

  from which the good

  draws lessons.

If honouring not one's teacher,

Or loving not one's material，

One is a big fool

  though he seems clever.

Here lies the vital secret.

二十八章

zhī qí xióng
知其雄，

shǒu qí cí
守其雌，

wéi tiān xià xī
爲天下谿。

wéi tiān xià xī
爲天下谿，

cháng dé bù lí
常德不離，

fù guī yú yīng ér
復歸於嬰兒。

zhī qí bái
知其白，

shǒu qí hēi
守其黑，

wéi tiān xià shì
爲天下式。

cháng dé bù tè
常德不忒，

Chapter 28

Though knowing what is masculine,
You are ready to play the role of female
And content to be a stream in the world.
Content to be a stream in the world,
You will be accompanied
    by the eternal virtue,
And return to being a baby.
Though knowing what is white,
You are ready to play the role of black,
And content to be a model of the world.
Content to be a model of the world,
You will be no longer at odds
    with the eternal virtue,

fù guī yú wú jí
復歸於無極。

zhī qí róng
知其榮，

shǒu qí rǔ
守其辱，

wéi tiān xià gǔ
爲天下谷。

wéi xià xià gǔ
爲下下谷，

cháng dé nǎi zú
常德乃足，

fù guī yú pǔ
復歸於樸。

pǔ sàn zé wéi qì
樸散則爲器，

shèng rén yòng zhī
聖人用之，

zé wéi guān zhǎng
則爲官長。

gù
故

dà zhì bù gē
大制不割。

And return to the final truth.

Though knowing what is honor,

You are ready to play the role

    of the disgraced

And content to be a valley in the world.

Content to be a valley in the world,

You will no longer lack the eternal virtue,

    And return to Simplicity (Tao).

When Simplicity gets shattered

    and becomes materialized,

The sage makes use of it to be the lord

    over other officials.

One should know

The greatest system is not separable.

二十九章

jiāng yù qǔ tiān xià ér wéi zhī
將欲取天下而爲之，

wú jiàn qí bù dé yǐ
吾見其不得已。

tiān xià shén qì
天下神器，

bù kě wéi yě
不可爲也。

wéi zhě bài zhī
爲者敗之，

zhí zhě shī zhī
執者失之。

fú wù
夫物

huò xíng huò suí
或行或隨，

huò xū huò chuī
或歔或吹，

huò qiáng huò léi
或强或羸，

huò zài huò huī
或載或隳。

shì yǐ
是以

shèng rén qù shèn qù shē qù tài
聖人去甚去奢去泰。

Chapter 29

He who wants to gain the kingship by force

Can never be successful, I think.

The kingship is so sacred

That cannot be obtained through force.

Those who try to obtain it by force will ruin it;

Those who keep it by force will lose it.

All things under Heaven

Either go ahead or follow;

Either breathe gently or hard;

Either are strong or weak;

Either are in safety or in danger.

Hence the sage does away with extremity,

extravagance and excess.

三十章

以道佐人主者，
yǐ dào zuǒ rén zhǔ zhě

不以兵强天下，
bù yǐ bīng qiáng tiān xià

其事好還：
qí shì hào huán

師之所處，荆棘生焉，
shī zhī suǒ chǔ   jīng jí shēng yān

大軍之後，必有凶年。
dà jūn zhī hòu   bì yǒu xiōng nián

善者果而已，
shàn zhě guǒ ér yǐ

不敢以取强。
bù gǎn yǐ qǔ qiáng

果而勿矜，
guǒ ér wù jīn

果而勿伐，
guǒ ér wù fá

果而勿驕，
guǒ ér wù jiāo

Chapter 30

He who assists the ruler
　　by means of Tao
Does not conquer other countries
　　by the military force.
Military actions usually invite
　　retaliatory aftermath：
Wherever armies station,
Thistles and thorns grow;
A great war is always followed
By a great famine.
He who is well versed in the art of war
Only uses the force to win the war,
And not to bully or conquer
　　other countries.
Win the war but do not boast；
Win the war but do not brag；
Win the war but do not show arrogance；

guǒ ér bù dé yǐ
果 而 不 得 已，

guǒ ér wù qiáng
果 而 勿 强 。

wù zhuàng zé lǎo
物 壮 则 老，

shì wèi bù dào
是 谓 不 道，

bù dào zǎo yǐ
不 道 早 已。

道 德 经

Win the war but do know
    it is out of necessity;
Win the war but do not thereby
    bully and conquer other countries.
Whatever is in its prime is bound to decline;
For, being in prime is against Tao;
Whatever goes against Tao
Will come to an early end.

○八七

三十一章

fú bīng zhě bù xiáng zhī qì
夫兵者不祥之器，

wù huò wù zhī
物或恶之，

gù yǒu dào zhě bù chǔ
故有道者不處。

jūn zǐ jū zé guì zuǒ
君子居則貴左，

yòng bīng zé guì yòu
用兵則貴右。

bīng zhě bù xiáng zhī qì
兵者不祥之器，

fēi jūn zǐ zhī qì
非君子之器，

bù dé yǐ ér yòng zhī
不得已而用之，

tián dàn wéi shàng
恬淡爲上。

shèng ér bù měi
勝而不美。

Chapter 31

Weapons are tools of ill omen,

Detested by everybody.

And a man of Tao does not use them.

The gentleman usually favours the left,*

But when being at war, he favours the right.*

Weapons are tools of ill omen,

Not the instruments of the gentleman.

Even if compelled to use them,

The gentleman does not use them with pleasure.

Even if being the victor,

The gentleman does not glorify the victory.

---

* Ancient Chinese thought the left stood for the Yang
(positive, male, etc.), while the right for the Yin
(negative, passive, female, etc.).

ér měi zhī zhě
而美之者。

shì lè shā rén
是樂殺人。

fú lè shā rén zhě
夫樂殺人者，

bù kě yǐ dé zhì yú tiān xià yǐ
不可以得志於天下矣。

jí shì shàng zuǒ
吉事尚左，

xiōng shì shàng yòu
凶事尚右。

piān jiāng jūn jū zuǒ
偏將軍居左，

shàng jiāng jūn jū yòu
上將軍居右，

yán yǐ sāng lǐ chǔ zhī
言以喪禮處之。

shā rén zhī zhòng
殺人之眾，

yǐ āi bēi qì zhī
以哀悲泣之，

zhàn shèng yǐ sāng lǐ chǔ zhī
戰勝以喪禮處之。

He who glorifies the victory

Is one who takes delight in killing.

He who takes delight in killing

Can never be successful in winning the empire.

On occasions of auspicious celebration

    the left is favoured;

On occasions of mourning

    the right is favoured.

A lieutenant's position is on the left;

A general's position is on the right.

That is to say, mourning rites

    should be observed in military operations.

War brings about heavy casualties,

So one should take part in it with deep sorrow.

When winning the victory, victors should treat

    the dead by observing the rites of mourning.

三十二章

dào cháng wú míng
道 常 無 名。

pǔ suī xiǎo
樸 雖 小 ，＊

tiān xià mò néng chén yě
天 下 莫 能 臣 也。

hóu wáng ruò néng shǒu zhī
侯 王 若 能 守 之 ，

wàn wù jiāng zì bīn
萬 物 將 自 賓。

tiān dì xiāng hé
天 地 相 合 ，

yǐ jiàng gān lù
以 降 甘 露 ，

mín mò zhī lìng ér zì jūn
民 莫 之 令 而 自 均。

shǐ zhì yǒu míng
始 制 有 名。

míng yì jì yǒu
名 亦 既 有 ，

fú yì jiāng zhī zhǐ
夫 亦 將 知 止。

zhī zhǐ kě yǐ bù dài
知 止 可 以 不 殆。

pì dào zhī zài tiān xià
譬 道 之 在 天 下 ，

yóu chuān gǔ zhī yú jiāng hǎi
猶 川 谷 之 於 江 海。

＊ 郭店楚簡：仆唯妻。

Chapter 32

Tao is nameless for ever.
Though it is very small,*
It is subject to no one in the world.
They can bring all things in the world
    under subjection.
When Yin and Yang
    between Heaven and Earth unite,
Sweet dew will fall,
    so equally scattered down
Without any interference
    on the part of the people.
The administration of the empire
    demands names;
Names are once given,
Limitations are thereby known.
The knowledge of limitations
    helps avoid danger.
Tao is to the world
    what the river and the sea
Are to the countless streamlets.

○
九
三

---

* Guodian Chu Slips: though the Pu (Tao) is
very small

三十三章

zhī rén zhě zhì
知人者智，

zì zhī zhě míng
自知者明。

shèng rén zhě yǒu lì
勝人者有力，

zì shèng zhě qiáng
自勝者强。

zhī zú zhě fù
知足者富，

qiáng xíng zhě yǒu zhì
强行者有志，

bù shī qí suǒ zhě jiǔ
不失其所者久，

sǐ ér bù wáng zhě shòu
死而不亡者壽。

Chapter 33

He who knows others is wise;

He who knows himself is clever;

He who conquers others is forceful;

He who conquers himself is powerful;

He who knows contentment is rich;

He who perseveres is a man of will;

He who does not lose his root can endure;

He whose Tao survives him is long–lived.

三十四章

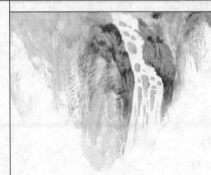

dà dào fàn xī
大 道 泛 兮，

　　qí kě zuǒ yòu
　　其 可 左 右。

wàn wù shì zhī yǐ shēng ér bù cí
萬 物 恃 之 以 生 而 不 辭，

gōng chéng bù míng yǒu
功 成 不 名 有。

yī yǎng wàn wù ér bù wéi zhǔ
衣 養 萬 物 而 不 爲 主，

kě míng yú xiǎo
可 名 於 小；

wàn wù guī yān ér bù wéi zhǔ
萬 物 歸 焉 而 不 爲 主，

kě míng wéi dà
可 名 爲 大。

yǐ qí zhōng bù zì wéi dà
以 其 終 不 自 爲 大，

gù néng chéng qí dà
故 能 成 其 大。

Chapter 34

The great Tao is felt everywhere

Extending in all directions.

All things grow on it

    and it never declines them.

It accomplishes its great task

    without claiming to merit.

It breeds all things

    without claiming to be their master;

It can be called Small.

All thing finally return to it

And it never claims to be their master;

And it can be called Great.

It becomes Great

Because it never claims to be Great.

三十五章

zhí dà xiàng
執 大 象 ，

tiān xià wǎng
天 下 往 。

wǎng ér bù hài
往 而 不 害 ，

ān píng tài
安 平 泰 。

yuè yǔ ěr
樂 與 餌 ，

guò kè zhǐ
過 客 止 。

dào zhī chū kǒu
道 之 出 口 ，

dàn hū qí wú wèi
淡 乎 其 無 味 ，

shì zhī bù zú jiàn
視 之 不 足 見 ，

tīng zhī bù zú wén
聽 之 不 足 聞 ，

yòng zhī bù zú jì
用 之 不 足 既 。

Chapter 35

He who holds the great image (Tao)

Attracts all the people to him.

Coming to him and not harming each other,

They all live in peace and happiness.

Music and food

Can allure passersby to stop,

But Tao, coming out of the mouth,

Is tasteless.

It cannot be seen,

It cannot be heard,

But when using it,

     you can never exhaust its use.

三十六章

jiāng yù xī zhī
將　欲　歙　之，
　　　bì gù zhāng zhī
　　　必　固　張　之；

jiāng yù ruò zhī
將　欲　弱　之，
　　　bì gù qiáng zhī
　　　必　固　强　之；

jiāng yù fèi zhī
將　欲　廢　之，
　　　bì gù xīng zhī
　　　必　固　興　之；

jiāng yù duó zhī
將　欲　奪　之，
　　　bì gù yǔ zhī
　　　必　固　與　之。

shì wèi wēi míng
是　謂　微　明，
róu ruò shèng gāng qiáng
柔　弱　勝　剛　强。
yú bù kě tuō yú yuān
魚　不　可　脫　於　淵，
guó zhī lì qì
國　之　利　器
　　　bù kě yǐ shì rén
　　　不　可　以　示　人。

Chapter 36

If you want a thing to contract,

You should stretch it first;

If you want a thing weakened,

You should strengthen it first;

If you want a thing gotten rid of,

You should promote it first;

If you want to be a taker,

You should be a giver first.

These are called subtle wisdom.

The supple and weak overcomes

    the rigid and strong.

Fish should not be allowed

    to leave the deep water;

The instruments of power of a state

Should not be shown to the public.

三十七章

dào cháng wú wéi
道 常 無 爲 ，
　　　ér wú bù wéi
　　而 無 不 爲 。

hóu wáng ruò néng shǒu zhī
侯 王 若 能 守 之 ，
wàn wù jiāng zì huà
萬 物 將 自 化 。

huà ér yù zuò
化 而 欲 作 ，
wú jiāng zhèn zhī yǐ wú míng zhī pǔ
吾 將 鎮 之 以 無 名 之 樸 。

zhèn zhī yǐ wú míng zhī pǔ
鎮 之 以 無 名 之 樸 ，
　　　fú jiāng wú yù
　　夫 將 无 欲 。

bù yù yǐ jìng
不 欲 以 静 ，
　　　tiān xià jiāng zì dìng
　　天 下 將 自 定 。

Chapter 37

Tao always remains inactive,

Yet it acts upon everything in the world.

If lords and kings can keep it,

All creatures will grow and develop naturally.

When desires are kindled

    in the growth and development,

I can suppress them

    with the nameless Simplicity

    of Tao.

Once I do so

Desires will be repressed.

Once desires are repressed,

The whole world will be naturally at peace.

一〇三

德 经

The Book of Teh

三十八章

shàng dé bù dé
上 德不德，

shì yǐ yǒu dé
是 以 有 德 。

xià dé bù shī dé
下 德不失德，

shì yǐ wú dé
是 以 無 德 。

shàng dé wú wéi ér wú yǐ wéi
上 德 無 爲 而 無 以 爲 。

xià dé wú wéi ér yǒu yǐ wéi
下 德 無 爲 而 有 以 爲 。

shàng rén wéi zhī ér wú yǐ wéi
上 仁 爲 之 而 無 以 爲 。

shàng yì wéi zhī ér yǒu yǐ wéi
上 義 爲 之 而 有 以 爲 。

shàng lǐ wéi zhī ér mò zhī yìng
上 禮 爲 之 而 莫 之 應 ，

zé rǎng bì ér rēng zhī
則 攘 臂 而 扔 之 。

Chapter 38

A man of the great virtue (Teh)*

 does not claim to be of virtue,

Thus he is of the true virtue.

A man of the small virtue

 always holds fast to the virtue in form.

Thus he is actually of no virtue.

A man of the great virtue remains inactive,

Without deliberately manifesting his virtue;

A man of the small benevolence

 keeps being active,

Always deliberately manifesting his virtue.

A man of the great benevolence acts

 but never deliberately

 shows his benevolence;

A man of great justice acts

 and also deliberately shows his justice.

A man of rigid rites acts

 and even rolls up his sleeves

to force people to conform to rites

 when no one responds to him.

一〇七

---

* Teh: spelled as "De" in Chinese phonetic
 symbols, meaning virtue.

gù
故

shī dào ér hòu dé
失 道 而 後 德，

shī dé ér hòu rén
失 德 而 後 仁，

shī rén ér hòu yì
失 仁 而 後 義，

shī yì ér hòu lǐ
失 義 而 後 禮。

fú lǐ zhě
夫 禮 者，

zhōng xìn zhī bó ér luàn zhī shǒu
忠 信 之 薄 而 亂 之 首。

qián shí zhě
前 識 者，

dào zhī huá ér yú zhī shǐ
道 之 華 而 愚 之 始。

shì yǐ dà zhàng fū
是 以 大 丈 夫

chǔ qí hòu　 bù jū qí bó
處 其 厚，不 居 其 薄，

chǔ qí shí　 bù jū qí huá
處 其 實，不 居 其 華。

gù qù bǐ gǔ cǐ
故 去 彼 取 此。

Therefore

Virtue comes after the loss of Tao;

Benevolence comes after the loss of virtue;

Justice comes after the loss of benevolence;

Rites come after the loss of justice.

Thus rites result from the lack of loyalty
    and good faith,

And function as the beginning
    of the great disorder.

Foresight is only the flowery embellishment
    of Tao

As well as the beginning of ignorance.

Hence the true man sets store by the thick
    rather than by the thin,

And values the fruit rather than the flower.

That is why he takes the former
    and discards the latter.

三十九章

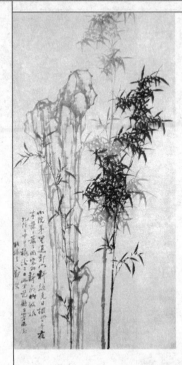

xī zhī dé yī zhě
昔之得一者——

tiān dé yī yǐ qīng
天 得 一 以 清 ，

dì dé yī yǐ níng
地 得 一 以 寧 ，

shén dé yī yǐ líng
神 得 一 以 靈 ，

gǔ dé yī yǐ yíng
谷 得 一 以 盈 ，

wàn wù dé yī yǐ shēng
萬 物 得 一 以 生 ，

hóu wáng dé yī yǐ wéi tiān xià zhèng
侯 王 得 一 以 爲 天 下 正 。

qí zhì zhī yě
其 致 之 也 ，

tiān wú yǐ qīng   jiāng kǒng liè
天 無 以 清 ， 將 恐 裂 ；

dì wú yǐ níng   jiāng kǒng fā
地 無 以 寧 ， 將 恐 發 ；

shén wú yǐ líng   jiāng kǒng xiē
神 無 以 靈 ， 將 恐 歇 ；

Chapter 39

Among the ancient holders of the One (Tao):
Heaven that holds the One becomes
    clear and bright;
Earth that holds the One becomes steady;
Gods that hold the One become efficacious;
Valleys that hold the One become full;
All creatures that hold the One become alive;
Lords and leaders who hold the One become
    leaders of the human world.
By inference
Heaven might split
    without what makes it clear and bright;
Earth might shake
    without what makes it steady;
Gods might disappear
    without what makes it efficacious;

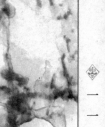

gǔ wú yǐ yíng　jiāng kǒng jié
谷 無 以 盈 ， 將 恐 竭 ；

wàn wù wú yǐ chōng　jiāng kǒng miè
萬 物 無 以 生 ， 將 恐 滅 ；

hóu wáng wú yǐ guì gāo　jiāng kǒng jué
侯 王 無 以 貴 高 ， 將 恐 蹶 。

gù
故

guì yǐ jiàn wéi běn
貴 以 賤 爲 本 ，

gāo yǐ xià wéi jī
高 以 下 爲 基 。

shì yǐ hóu wáng zì wèi gū　guǎ　bù gǔ
是 以 侯 王 自 謂 孤 、 寡 、 不 穀 。

cǐ fēi yǐ jiàn wéi běn yé
此 非 以 賤 爲 本 耶 ？

fēi hū
非 乎 ？

gù
故

zhì yù wú yù
至 譽 無 譽 。

bù yù lù lù rú yù
不 欲 瑯 瑯 如 玉 ，

luò luò rú shí
珞 珞 如 石 。

Valleys might go dry

    without what makes it full;

All creatures might die out

    without what makes them alive;

Lords and kings might fall

    without what makes them leaders.

That is why the humble

    is the root of the noble,

And the high is based on the low.

That is why lords and kings

    call themselves

    "the solitary", "the few" and "the unkind".

Does not this take the humble as the root

    (of the noble)?

Does this not?

Hence the highest honor

    does not need honoring.

It is better, therefore,

    to be a hard stone than a beautiful

    piece of jade.

四十章

fǎn zhě dào zhī dòng
反 者 道 之 動 ，*

ruò zhě dào zhī yòng
弱 者 道 之 用 。

tiān xià wàn wù shēng yú yǒu
天 下 萬 物 生 於 有 ，

yǒu shēng yú wú
有 生 於 無 。**

＊ 郭店楚簡：返也者，道僮(動)也。

＊＊ 郭店楚簡：天下之勿(物)生於又(有)，生於亡(無)。

Chapter 40

Cycling is the movement of Tao;*
Being weak is the function of Tao.
All things of the world
    are born from Existence (Being),
And Being from Nothingness.**

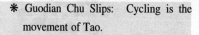

  ✳ Guodian Chu Slips: Cycling is the
    movement of Tao.
✳ ✳ Guodian Chu Slips: All things of the
    world are born from Existence
    (Being), / And are also born from
    Nothingness.

四十一章

shàng shì wén dào
上 士 聞 道，

    qín ér xíng zhī
    勤而行之。

zhōng shì wén dào
中 士 聞 道，

    ruò cún ruò wáng
    若存若 亡。

xià shì wén dào
下 士 聞 道，

    dà xiào zhī
    大 笑 之。

bù xiào bù zú yǐ wéi dào
不 笑 不 足 以 爲 道！

gù jiàn yán yǒu zhī
故 建 言 有 之：

    míng dào ruò mèi
    明 道 若 昧，

    jìn dào ruò tuì
    進 道 若 退，

    yí dào ruò lèi
    夷 道 若 纇，

Chapter 41

Hearing Tao, the best scholar
    assiduously practices it;
The average scholar
    half believes and half doubts it;
The worst scholar
    bursts into laughter about it.
If the worst scholar
    does not laugh about it,
Tao is not worthy
    of being called Tao.
That is why the ancients say:
The bright Tao seems dark;
The advancing Tao
    seems to be retreating;
The even Tao seems rough;

shàng dé ruò gǔ
上 德 若 谷 ,

dà bái ruò rǔ
大 白 若 辱 ,

guǎng dé ruò bù zú
廣 德 若 不 足 ,

jiàn dé ruò tōu
建 德 若 偷 ,

zhì zhēn ruò yú
質 真 若 渝 。

dà fāng wú yú
大 方 無 隅 ,

dà qì wǎn chéng
大 器 晚 成 , *

dà yīn xī shēng
大 音 希 聲 ,

dà xiàng wú xíng
大 象 無 形 。 **

dào yǐn wú míng
道 隱 無 名 ,

fū wéi dào   shàn dài qiě chéng
夫 唯 道 , 善 貸 且 成 。

一一八

* 郭店楚簡：大器曼（慢）成。
** 郭店楚簡：天象亡形。

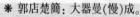

The great virtue resembles the valley;
The pure whiteness seems black;
The infinite virtue seems lacking;
The virile virtue seems idle;
The pure simplicity seems turbid.
The great square has no corners;
Of the utensils the most precious
    takes the longest time to be finished;*
The great sound seems soundless;
The great image seems formless.**
Tao always conceals itself
    without a name,
But it is Tao alone that helps
    and completes everything.

一一九

---

* Guodian Chu Slips: The most precious utensil slowly and
    gradually takes shape.

** Guodian Chu Slips: The image of heaven is formless.

四十二章

dào shēng yī
道 生 一，

yī shēng èr
一 生 二，

èr shēng sān
二 生 三，

sān shēng wàn wù
三 生 萬 物。

wàn wù fù yīn ér bào yáng
萬 物 負 陰 而 抱 陽，

chōng qì yǐ wéi hé
冲 氣 以 爲 和。

rén zhī suǒ wù
人 之 所 惡，

wéi gū guǎ bù gǔ
唯 孤、寡、不 穀。

ér wàng gōng yǐ wéi chēng
而 王 公 以 爲 稱。

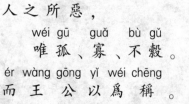

Chapter 42

Tao begets the One；

The One consists of Two in opposition

    (the Yin and Yang)；

The Two begets the Three；

The Three begets all things of the world.

All things connote the Yin and Yang.

The Yin and Yang keep acting

    upon each other

And thus things keep changing

    and unifying themselves.

Words like "the solitary"，

"the few" and "the unkind"

Are usually detested by people，

Yet lords and kings

    use them to call themselves.

gù wù
故物

huò sǔn zhī ér yì
或 损 之 而 益 ；

huò yì zhī ér sǔn
或 益 之 而 损 。

rén zhī suǒ jiào
人 之 所 教 ，

wǒ yì jiào zhī
我 亦 教 之 ：

qiáng liáng zhě bù dé qí sǐ
" 强 梁 者 不 得 其 死 " ，

wú jiāng yǐ wéi jiào fù
吾 将 以 爲 教 父 。

That is why

A thing is sometimes added to

    when being reduced,

Or is reduced when being added to.

So I teach what I am taught：

"The violent will not come to a good end."

This I will take as the first lesson when I teach.

四十三章

tiān xià zhī zhì róu
天 下 之 至 柔

chí chěng tiān xià zhī zhì jiān
馳 騁 天 下 之 至 堅。

wú yǒu rù wú jiān
無 有 入 無 間。

wú shì yǐ zhī wú wéi zhī yǒu yì
吾 是 以 知 無 爲 之 有 益。

bù yán zhī jiào
不 言 之 教,

wú wéi zhī yì
無 爲 之 益,

tiān xià xī jí zhī
天 下 希 及 之。

Chapter 43

The most supple in the world

Can go through the hardest in the world.

What consists of no substance

    can enter what has no crevices.

I thus know the benefit of inaction.

Teaching without words,

The benefit of inaction,

Are what few people in the world

    can perform and obtain.

四十四章

míng yǔ shēn shú qīn
名 与 身 孰 亲 ?

shēn yǔ huò shú duō
身 与 货 孰 多 ?

dé yǔ wáng shú bìng
得 与 亡 孰 病 ?

shèn ài bì dà fèi
甚 爱 必 大 费 ,

duō cáng bì hòu wáng
多 藏 必 厚 亡 。

gù zhī zú bù rǔ
故 知 足 不 辱 ,

zhī zhǐ bù dài
知 止 不 殆 ,

kě yǐ cháng jiǔ
可 以 长 久 。

Chapter 44

Which is dearer,
    your name or your body?
Which is more important,
    your body or your goods?
Which is more harmful,
    gain or loss?
Excessive stinginess will result
    in great expense;
Too much amassment
    leads to great loss;
Knowing contentment
    avoids disgrace;
Knowing when to stop
    avoids danger.
Thus one can be long in safety.

四十五章

dà chéng ruò quē
大 成 若 缺 ，

qí yòng bù bì
其 用 不 弊 。

dà yíng ruò chōng
大 盈 若 冲 ，

dà biàn ruò nè
大 辩 若 讷 。 *

qí yòng bù qióng
其 用 不 窮 。

zào shèng hán
躁 勝 寒 ，

dà zhí ruò qū
大 直 若 屈 ，

jìng shèng rè
静 勝 热 ，

dà qiǎo ruò zhuō
大 巧 若 拙 ，

qīng jìng wéi tiān xià zhèng
清 静 爲 天 下 正 。

＊ 郭店楚簡：大成若詘。

Chapter 45

The complete perfection seems flawed,

But its use can never be exhausted;

The fullest seems empty,

But its use can never come to an end;

The straightest seems bent;

The most skillful seems clumsy;

The most eloquent seems tongue-tied.*

Movement overcomes cold;

Quiet overcomes heat.

So inaction and quiet help one

Become a leader of the world.

* Guodian Chu Slips: The most successful seems slow in speech.

四十六章

tiān xià yǒu dào
天 下 有 道 ，

què zǒu mǎ yǐ fèn
却 走 馬 以 糞 。

tiān xià wú dào
天 下 無 道 ，

róng mǎ shēng yú jiāo
戎 馬 生 於 郊 。

huò mò dà yú bù zhī zú
禍 莫 大 於 不 知 足 ，

jiù mò dà yú yù dé
咎 莫 大 於 欲 得 。 *

gù
故

zhī zú zhī zú
知 足 之 足 ，

cháng zú yǐ
常 足 矣 。

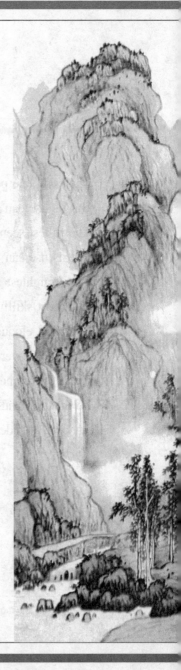

---

* 郭店楚簡：罪莫厚乎甚欲，咎莫
憯乎欲得

Chapter 46

When Tao prevails in the world,
The battle steeds are turned
    to farmers for tilling the fields;
When Tao does not prevail
    in the world,
Even pregnant mares
    are taken over for wars.*
No crime is greater than greediness;
No disaster is greater
    than the lack of contentment;
Thus the contentment of feeling content
Is an eternal contentment.

---

* Guodian Chu Slips: No crime is greater than
  indulgence in sensual pleasures, / No danger
  is greater than greediness.

四十七章

bù chū hù
不 出 户 ，

zhī tiān xià
知 天 下 。

bù kuī yǒu
不 窥 牖 ，

jiàn tiān dào
见 天 道 。

qí chū mí yuǎn
其 出 弥 远 ，

qí zhī mí shǎo
其 知 弥 少 。

shì yǐ shèng rén
是 以 圣 人

bù xíng ér zhī
不 行 而 知 。

bù jiàn ér míng
不 见 而 名 ，

bù wéi ér chéng
不 为 而 成 。

Chapter 47

Without stirring out of the house,

One can know everything in the world;

Without looking out of the window,

One can see Tao of heaven.

The further one travels,

The less one knows.

That is why the sage

Knows everything without going out;

Sees Tao of heaven

    without looking out of the window;

Succeeds without resorting to action.

四十八章

wéi xué rì yì
爲 學 日 益 ,

wéi dào rì sǔn
爲 道 日 損 ,

sǔn zhī yòu sǔn
損 之 又 損 ,

yǐ zhì yú wú wéi
以 至 於 無 爲 。

wú wéi ér wú bù wéi
無 爲 而 無 不 爲 。

qǔ tiān xià cháng yǐ wú shì
取 天 下 常 以 無 事 。

jí qí yǒu shì
及 其 有 事 ,

bù zú yǐ qǔ tiān xià
不 足 以 取 天 下 。

Chapter 48

He who seeks learning

    must increase his knowledge every day;

He who seeks Tao

    must reduce his knowledge every day;

He reduces and reduces

    until he reaches the state of inaction.

When reaching the state of inaction,

    one can succeed in everything.

To govern the world well,

    one must take inaction as the principle.

If one governs with too much action,

    one is not a worthy governor.

四十九章

shèng rén wú cháng xīn
聖人無常心，

　　yǐ bǎi xìng xīn wéi xīn
　　以百姓心爲心。

shàn zhě wú shàn zhī
善者吾善之，

bù shàn zhě wú yì shàn zhī
不善者吾亦善之，

dé shàn
德善。

xìn zhě wú xìn zhī
信者吾信之，

bù xìn zhě wú yì xìn zhī
不信者吾亦信之，

dé xìn
德信。

Chapter 49

The sage often has no will,
He takes the people's will as his own.
What is good
    I treat with goodness.
What is not good
    I also treat with goodness;
Thus I obtain goodness.
Those who are of faith,
    I put faith in;
Those who are of no faith,
    I also put faith in.
Thus I obtain faith.

shèng rén zài tiān xià
聖 人 在 天 下，

xī xī yān
歙 歙 焉；

wéi tiān xià hún qí xīn
爲 天 下 渾 其 心，

bǎi xìng jiē zhù qí ěr mù
百 姓 皆 注 其 耳 目。

shèng rén jiē hái zhī
聖 人 皆 孩 之。

When the sage governs the world,
He weakens his will
    and simplifies the people's minds.
The people are all preoccupied
    with their eyes and ears,
The sage helps them return
    to the childhood state.

五十章

chū shēng rù sǐ
出 生 入 死。

shēng zhī tú shí yǒu sān
生 之 徒 十 有 三,

sǐ zhī tú shí yǒu sān
死 之 徒 十 有 三,

rén zhī shēng　dòng zhī yú sǐ dì
人 之 生, 動 之 於 死 地

yì shí yǒu sān
亦 十 有 三。

fú hé gù
夫 何 故?

yǐ qí shēng shēng zhī hòu
以 其 生 生 之 厚。

gài wén shàn shè shēng zhě
蓋 聞 善 攝 生 者,

lù xíng bù yù sì hǔ
陸 行 不 遇 兕 虎,

rù jūn bù bèi jiǎ bīng
入 軍 不 被 甲 兵,

Chapter 50

When given to birth men live

And when being buried they die.

One third of them are long-lived;

One third of them are short-lived;

One third of them die

    from their own choices

    though they could have lived longer.

Why in such cases?

Because they are too eager to live longer;

It is heard

    that he who is good at preserving his life

Does not meet with the rhinoceros

    or tiger when traveling on land,

Nor is he wounded in war,

sì wú suǒ tóu qí jiǎo
兕無所投其角，

hǔ wú suǒ cuò qí zhǎo
虎無所措其爪，

bīng wú suǒ róng qí rèn
兵無所容其刃，

fú hé gù
夫何故？

yǐ qí wú sǐ dì
以其無死地。

So the rhinoceros has no use for its horns
And the tiger has no use for its claws;
The weapons have no use for their blades.
Why in such cases?
Because there is no realm of death
     for him to enter.

五十一章

dào shēng zhī
道 生 之 ，

dé xù zhī
德 畜 之 ，

wù xíng zhī
物 形 之 ，

shì chéng zhī
势 成 之 。

shì yǐ wàn wù mò bù zūn dào ér guì dé
是 以 萬 物 莫 不 尊 道 而 貴 德 。

dào zhī zūn
道 之 尊 ，

dé zhī guì
德 之 貴 ，

fú mò zhī mìng ér cháng zì rán
夫 莫 之 命 而 常 自 然 。

gù
故

dào shēng zhī
道 生 之 ，

Chapter 51

Tao begets all creatures;

Teh (virtue) rears them;

Substance gives them shape;

Forces in opposition accomplish them.

Therefore all creatures

     worship Tao and honor Teh.

This worship and honor stems from the fact

That Tao and Teh (virtue) never unnaturally

Impose their influence on all creatures.

In this way

Tao begets all creatures;

dé xù zhī
德畜之，

zhǎng zhī yù zhī
長之育之，

tíng zhī dú zhī
亭之毒之，

yǎng zhī fù zhī
養之覆之。

shēng ér bù yǒu
生而不有，

wéi ér bù shì
爲而不恃，

zhǎng ér bù zǎi
長而不宰，

shì wèi xuán dé
是謂玄德。

Teh (virtue) rears them,

Promotes them, nutures them,

Brings them to fruition and maturity,

Meanwhile maintains and defends them.

Giving them life

　　without claiming to be their owner;

Availing them

　　without claiming to be their benefactor;

And being their head

　　without ruling them;

All these are called

　　the most intrinsic Teh (virtue).

五十二章

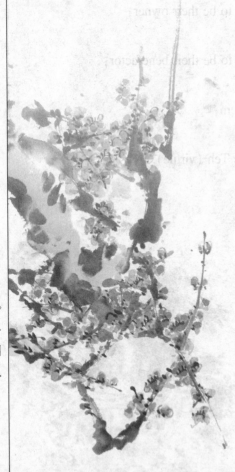

tiān xià yǒu shǐ
天下有始，

yǐ wéi tiān xià mǔ
以爲天下母。

jì dé qí mǔ
既得其母，

yǐ zhī qí zǐ
以知其子。

jì zhī qí zǐ
既知其子，

fù shǒu qí mǔ
復守其母，

mò shēn bù dài
没身不殆。

sè qí duì
塞其兑，

bì qí mén
閉其門，

zhōng shēn bù qín
終身不勤。

Chapter 52

The universe has a beginning (Tao);
The beginning functions
    as the mother of all things.
If you know the mother,
You get to know her children
    (all things);
If, while knowing the children,
You keep the mother,
You will be a sage all your life.
Block the openings (of knowledge),
Shut the door (of desires),
And you will be free from illness
    all your life.

kāi qí duì
開其兌，

jì qí shì
濟其事，

zhōng shēn bù jiù
終　身　不　救。

jiàn xiǎo yuē míng
見　小　日　明，

shǒu róu yuē qiáng
守　柔　日　强。

yòng qí guāng
用　其　光，

fù guī qí míng
復歸其明，

wú yí shēn yāng
無　遺　身　殃，

shì wéi xí cháng
是　爲　襲　常。

Unlock the openings,

Add to your cares,

And you will be incurable all your life.

To be able to perceive the minute

　　is called Discernment;

To be able to play the role of the weak

　　is called Strong.

Use the light

To return to the intrinsic discernment

And you will be free from disasters.

This is called the eternal Tao.

五十三章

shǐ wǒ jiè rán yǒu zhī
使我介然有知，

xíng yú dà dào
行於大道，

wéi yǐ shì wèi
惟施是畏。

dà dào shèn yí
大道甚夷，

ér mín hào jìng
而民好徑。

zhāo shèn chú
朝甚除，

tián shèn wú
田甚蕪，

cāng shèn xū
倉甚虛，

fú wén cǎi
服文彩，

dài lì jiàn
帶利劍，

yàn yǐn shí
厭飲食，

cái huò yǒu yú
財貨有餘，

shì wèi dào yú
是謂盜竽。

fēi dào yě zāi
非道也哉！

Chapter 53

If I have acquired a little knowledge,

I will be afraid of going astray

When I walk on the road.

The road is even,

Yet people prefer to take by-paths.

While the court is corrupt,

The fields lie waste;

The granaries are empty;

There are persons

who are still dressed gaudily,

Wearing ornamented swords,

Satiated with fine food and drink,

In possession of extravagant goods.

They can be called

the chieftains of robbers.

What a phenomenon against Tao!

五十四章

shàn jiàn zhě bù bá
善 建 者 不 拔，

shàn bào zhě bù tuō
善 抱 者 不 脱，

zǐ sūn yǐ jì sì bù chuò
子 孙 以 祭 祀 不 輟 。

xiū zhī yú shēn
修 之 於 身 ，

　　qí dé nǎi zhēn
　　其 德 乃 真 ；

xiū zhī yú jiā
修 之 於 家 ，

　　qí dé nǎi yú
　　其 德 乃 餘 ；

xiū zhī yú xiāng
修 之 於 鄉 ，

　　qí dé nǎi cháng
　　其 德 乃 長 ；

xiū zhī yú guó
修 之 於 國 ，

　　qí dé nǎi fēng
　　其 德 乃 豐 ；

Chapter 54

What is well planted cannot be pulled out;

What is well held cannot be disengaged;

The principle being observed,

The offering of sacrifice by descendants

　　will be kept for ever.

Applying the same principle to oneself,

One can purify his virtue;

Applying the same principle to one's family,

One makes his own virtue more than enough;

Applying the same principle to one's village,

One can have the virtue to be the leader;

Applying the same principle to one's state,

One can have the prodigious virtue;

xiū zhī yú tiān xià
修之於天下，

qí dé nǎi pǔ
其德乃普。

gù
故

yǐ shēn guān shēn
以身觀身，

yǐ jiā guān jiā
以家觀家，

yǐ xiāng guān xiāng
以鄉觀鄉，

yǐ guó guān guó
以國觀國，

yǐ tiān xià guān tiān xià
以天下觀天下，

wú hé yǐ zhī tiān xià rán zāi
吾何以知天下然哉？

yǐ cǐ
以此。

Applying the same principle to one's empire,

One can have the virtue widely known.

Hence I can have an insight

Into other individuals by examining myself;

Into other families by examining my family;

Into other villages by examining my village;

Into other states by examining my state;

Into other empires by examining my empire.

How do I know about the whole world?

By employing the method above.

五十五章

hán dó zhī hòu
含 德 之 厚 ，

bǐ yú chì zǐ
比 於 赤 子 。

dú chóng bù shì
毒 蟲 不 螫 ，

měng shòu bù jù
猛 獸 不 據 。

jué niǎo bù bó
攫 鳥 不 搏 。

gǔ ruò jīn róu ér wò gù
骨 弱 筋 柔 而 握 固 。

wèi zhī pìn mǔ zhī hé ér zuī zuò
未 知 牝 牡 之 合 而 朘 作 ，

jīng zhī zhì yě
精 之 至 也 。

zhōng rì háo ér bù shà
終 日 號 而 不 嗄 ，

hé zhī zhì yě
和 之 至 也 。

Chapter 55

A man of prodigious virtue

    is just like a newly-born baby：

Poisonous insects will not harm it；

Beasts of prey will not sting it；

Birds of prey will not swoop down upon it.

Its bones and muscles are weak and supple，

Yet its hold is tight.

It does not know sexual intercourse

    between the male and female，

Yet its little penis often erects itself；

This is because it is at the height of virility.

It cries all day long，

Yet its throat does not become hoarse；

This is because it is at the height

    of harmonious vim and vigor.

zhī hé yuē cháng
知 和 曰 常 ，*

zhī cháng yuē míng
知 常 曰 明 。

yì shēng yuē xiáng
益 生 曰 祥 ，

xīn shǐ qì yuē qiáng
心 使 氣 曰 強 。

wù zhuàng zé lǎo
物 壯 則 老 ，

wèi zhī bù dào
謂 之 不 道 ，

bù dào zǎo yǐ
不 道 早 已 。

---

* 郭店楚簡：智（知）和曰明。

To know harmony
   is to know the law of unity;*
To know the law of unity
   is to know discernment.
To indulge in sensual pleasures
   is to look for disasters;
To let virility driven by desires
   is to give free rein to strength.
A creature in its prime
   is at the turning-point of being old,
For it is against Tao.
What is against Tao
   comes to an early end.

---

* Guodian Chu Slips: To know
   harmony is to know discernment.

五十六章

zhì zhě bù yán
知 者 不 言，

yán zhě bù zhī
言 者 不 知，*

sè qí duì
塞 其 兑，

bì qí mén
閉 其 門，

cuò qí ruì
挫 其 銳，

jiě qí fēn
解 其 紛，

hé qí guāng
和 其 光，

tóng qí chén
同 其 塵，

shì wèi xuán tóng
是 謂 玄 同 。

gù
故

bù kě dé ér qīn
不 可 得 而 親，

bù kě dé ér shū
不 可 得 而 疏 。

bù kě dé ér lì
不 可 得 而 利，

bù kě dé ér hài
不 可 得 而 害 。

bù kě dé ér guì
不 可 得 而 貴，

bù kě dé ér jiàn
不 可 得 而 賤 。

gù wéi tiān xià guì
故 爲 天 下 貴 。

* 郭店楚簡：智之者弗言，言之者弗智。

Chapter 56

He who is wise will not speak;
He who speaks is not wise.*
When one blocks the openings
　(of knowledge),
Shuts the door (of desires),
Dulls sharpness,
Stays away from entanglements,
Glows with veiled radiance,
Mingles with dust,
That is called Subtle Identification.
Hence you are in no way
To be friends with him,
To estrange him,
To benefit him,
To harm him,
To honor him,
To debase him.
That is why he is held in esteem
　in the world.

一六三

---

* Guodian Chu Slips: He who is wise will not
speak; / he who speaks is not wise.
Translators note: "智" equals "知" in meaning
here. The Guodian Chu Slips confirms my
old translation.

五十七章

yǐ zhèng zhì guó
以 正 治 國，

yǐ qí yòng bīng
以 奇 用 兵，

yǐ wú shì qǔ tiān xià
以 無 事 取 天 下。

wú hé yǐ zhī qí rán zāi
吾 何 以 知 其 然 哉？

yǐ cǐ
以 此：

tiān xià duō jì huì ér mín mí pín
天 下 多 忌 諱 而 民 彌 貧；

mín duō lì qì guó jiā zī hūn
民 多 利 器，國 家 滋 昏；

rén duō jì qiǎo qí wù zī qǐ
人 多 伎 巧，奇 物 滋 起；

fǎ lìng zī zhāng dào zéi duō yǒu
法 令 滋 彰，盜 賊 多 有。

Chapter 57

Rule the state with peace and inaction;

Wage a war with crafty tricks;

Governing the world

    by not troubling the people.

How do I know it is the right way?

The reason is as follows:

The more prohibitions there are

    in the world,

The poorer the people are;

The more weapons the people own,

The more chaotic the state is;

The more skills the people have,

The more strange things occur;

The more laws and orders are issued,

The more thieves and robbers there are.

gù shèng rén yún
故 聖 人 云：

wǒ wú wéi ér mín zì huà
"我 無 爲 而 民 自 化。

wǒ hào jìng ér mín zì zhèng
我 好 静 而 民 自 正，

wǒ wú shì ér mín zì fù
我 無 事 而 民 自 富，

wǒ wú yù ér mín zì pǔ
我 無 欲 而 民 自 樸。"

Thus the sage says,

If I prefer inaction,

The people will naturally crave for peace;

If I act little,

The people will be naturally rectified;

If I am not meddlesome,

The people will naturally become rich;

If I get rid of desires,

The people will naturally become simple.

五十八章

其政<ruby>闷<rt>mèn</rt></ruby><ruby>闷<rt>mèn</rt></ruby>，
　其民<ruby>淳<rt>chún</rt></ruby><ruby>淳<rt>chún</rt></ruby>。

其政<ruby>察<rt>chá</rt></ruby><ruby>察<rt>chá</rt></ruby>，
　其民<ruby>缺<rt>quē</rt></ruby><ruby>缺<rt>quē</rt></ruby>。

<ruby>祸<rt>huò</rt></ruby><ruby>兮<rt>xī</rt></ruby>，<ruby>福<rt>fú</rt></ruby><ruby>之<rt>zhī</rt></ruby><ruby>所<rt>suǒ</rt></ruby><ruby>倚<rt>yǐ</rt></ruby>，

<ruby>福<rt>fú</rt></ruby><ruby>兮<rt>xī</rt></ruby>，<ruby>祸<rt>huò</rt></ruby><ruby>之<rt>zhī</rt></ruby><ruby>所<rt>suǒ</rt></ruby><ruby>伏<rt>fú</rt></ruby>。

<ruby>孰<rt>shú</rt></ruby><ruby>知<rt>zhī</rt></ruby><ruby>其<rt>qí</rt></ruby><ruby>极<rt>jí</rt></ruby>？

<ruby>其<rt>qí</rt></ruby><ruby>无<rt>wú</rt></ruby><ruby>正<rt>zhèng</rt></ruby><ruby>也<rt>yě</rt></ruby>。

　<ruby>正<rt>zhèng</rt></ruby><ruby>复<rt>fù</rt></ruby><ruby>为<rt>wéi</rt></ruby><ruby>奇<rt>qí</rt></ruby>，

　<ruby>善<rt>shàn</rt></ruby><ruby>复<rt>fù</rt></ruby><ruby>为<rt>wéi</rt></ruby><ruby>妖<rt>yāo</rt></ruby>，

Chapter 58

When the governor is magnanimous,
The people will become simple;
When the governor is harsh,
The people will become cunning.
Disaster hides itself behind good fortune;
Good fortune leans against disaster.
Who knows the secret?
There is no definite answer.
The normal may change into the abnormal;
The good may change into the evil.

rén zhī mí　qí rì gù jiǔ
人之迷，其日固久！

shì yǐ shèng rén
是以聖人

fāng ér bù gē
方而不割，

lián ér bù guì
廉而不劌，

zhí ér bù sì
直而不肆，

guāng ér bù yào
光而不耀。

People have been long perplexed.

Thus the sage is square and upright

But does not wound the people;

He is edged but does not cut the people;

He is candid but does not behave wantonly;

He gives light but does not dazzle.

五十九章

zhì rén shì tiān
治人事天，

　　mò ruò sè
　　莫若嗇。

fú wéi sè
夫唯嗇，

　　shì wèi zǎo fú
　　是謂早服。

zǎo fú wèi zhī zhòng jī dé
早服謂之重積德；

　zhòng jī dé zé wú bù kè
　重積德則無不克；

wú bù kè zé mò zhī qí jí
無不克則莫知其極。

mò zhī qí jí　kě yǐ yǒu guó
莫知其極，可以有國。

yǒu guó zhī mǔ　kě yǐ cháng jiǔ
有國之母，可以長久。

shì wèi
是謂

shēn gēn gù dǐ
深根固柢，

cháng shēng jiǔ shì zhī dào
長　生　久視之道。

Chapter 59

The best way to govern the state
  and keep in good health
Is to stint vitality.
To stint vitality means
  to attempt an early preparation;
The early preparation means
  to keep accumulating virtue;
Keep accumulating virtue
  and one can bcome all-conquering;
Be all-conquering
  and one's power will be beyond measure;
When one's power is beyond measure,
He can be entrusted with the duty
  of defending the state.
When there is the principle
  of governing the state,
The government can long endure.
This is called the Tao of deep roots
  and sturdy stems
By which one can enjoy a long life.

六十章

zhì dà guó ruò pēng xiǎo xiān
治大國若烹小鮮。

yǐ dào lì tiān xià
以道蒞天下，

　　qí guǐ bù shén
　　其鬼不神。

fēi qí guǐ bù shén
非其鬼不神，

　　qí shén bù shāng rén
　　其神不傷人。

fēi qí shén bù shāng rén
非其神不傷人，

　　shèng rén yì bù shāng rén
　　聖人亦不傷人，

fū liǎng bù xiāng shāng
夫兩不相傷，

　　gù dé jiāo guī yān
　　故德交歸焉。

Chapter 60

Ruling a large state resembles frying a small fish

(It is inappropriate to turn it over frequently).

When Tao prevails in the world,

Even ghosts and spirits become harmless.

It is not that ghosts really become harmless

But that their potencies

    can in no way harm people.

Not only ghosts become harmless,

Sages harm no people either.

Hence neither does any harm to the people

And both sages and ghosts

    help the people to enjoy the benefit of virtue.

六十一章

dà guó zhě xià liú
大國者卜流，

tiān xià zhī jiāo yě
天下之交也，

tiān xià zhī pìn
天下之牝。

pìn cháng yǐ jìng shèng mǔ
牝常以静勝牡，

　　yǐ jìng wéi xià
　　以静爲下。

gù dà guó yǐ xià xiǎo guó
故大國以下小國，

　　zé qǔ xiǎo guó
　　則取小國。

xiǎo guó yǐ xià dà guó
小國以下大國，

　　zé qǔ dà guó
　　則取大國。

gù
故

huò xià yǐ qǔ
或下以取，

huò xià ér qǔ
或下而取。

dà guó bù guò yù jiān xù rén
大國不過欲兼畜人，

xiǎo guó bù guò yù rù shì rén
小國不過欲入事人。

fū liǎng zhě gè dé qí suǒ yù
夫兩者各得其所欲，

dà zhě yí wéi xià
大者宜爲下。

Chapter 61

A large state should play the role of female,
Just like the lowest reaches of a river
Where all the other streams meet.
The female always conquers the male
　　　by motionlessness,
Because the motionless female
　　　always takes the lower position.
Hence the large state can annex the small one;
The small state can gain the trust of the large one
　　　by taking the lower position,
The case being either the former
　　　or vice versa.
The large state wants to put the small one
　　　under its protection,
The small state wants to be shielded
　　　by the large one,
Thus both can satisfy their own wishes,
After all, the large state should be more willing
　　　to take the lower position.

六十二章

dào zhě　　wàn wù zhī ào
道者，萬物之奧，

shàn rén zhī bǎo
善人之寶，

bù shàn rén zhī suǒ bǎo
不善人之所保。

měi yán kě yǐ shì zūn
美言可以市尊，

měi xíng kě yǐ jiā rén
美行可以加人。

rén zhī bù shàn
人之不善，

hé qì zhī yǒu
何棄之有？

gù
故

lì tiān zǐ
立天子，

zhì sān gōng
置三公，

Chapter 62

Tao is the innermost recess of all things;

It is what the good man cherishes

As well as what the bad man wants to keep.

With Tao, beautiful words can buy respect;

Beautiful deeds can be highly regarded.

How can the bad man desert Tao?

Hence when the emperor ascends the throne

    and appoints three ducal ministers,

suī yǒu gǒng bì
雖有拱璧

yǐ xiān sì mǎ
以先駟馬，

bù rú zuò jìn cǐ dào
不如坐進此道。

gǔ zhī suǒ yǐ guì cǐ dào zhě hé
古之所以貴此道者何？

bù yuē
不曰：

yǐ qiú dé
以求得，

yǒu zuì yǐ miǎn yé
有罪以免邪？

gù wéi tiān xià guì
故爲天下貴。

It would be better to present to the emperor

    Tao than jadewares

    followed by a team of four horses.

Why did ancients value Tao so much?

Was it not said that by making use of Tao

One could get what one desired

Or avoid punishment when committing an offense?

That is why it is valued so much in the world.

六十三章

wéi wú wéi
爲無爲，

shì wú shì
事無事，

wèi wú wèi
味無味。

dà xiǎo duō shǎo
大小多少，*

guó nán yú qí yì
國難於其易；

wéi dà yú qí xì
爲大於其細。

tiān xià nán shì
天下難事，

bì zuò yú yì
必作於易；

tiān xià dà shì
天下大事，

bì zuò yú xì
必作於細。

* 郭店楚簡：大，小之；

Chapter 63

Act by means of inaction;
Deal with matters by means
    of not being meddlesome;
Taste by means of tastelessness.
The big stems from the small;＊
The many is based on the few.
To overcome the difficult
    should begin with the easy;
To accomplish what is big
    should begin with the small.
The difficult things in the world
    must originate in the easy;
The big things in the world
    must take root in the small.

＊ Guodian Chu Slips: Belittle what is big;

shì yǐ shèng rén zhōng bù wéi dà
是以聖人終不爲大，

gù néng chéng qí dà
故能成其大。

fū qīng nuò bì guǎ xìn
夫輕諾必寡信，

duō yì bì duō nán
多易必多難。

shì yǐ shèng rén yóu nán zhī
是以聖人猶難之，

gù zhōng wú nán yǐ
故終無難矣。

That is why the sage can accomplish

    what is great by never attempting

    to be great.

Light promise-giving,

    light promise-breaking；

The easier one considers things，

    the more difficult things become.

That is why the sage

    never meets with difficulty

Because he always considers things difficult.

六十四章

qí ān yì chí
其 安 易 持 ；

qí wèi zhào yì móu
其 未 兆 易 谋 ；

qí cuì yì pàn
其 脆 易 泮 ；

qí wēi yì sàn
其 微 易 散 。

wéi zhī yú wèi yǒu
爲 之 於 未 有 ，

zhì zhī yú wèi luàn
治 之 於 未 亂 。

hé bào zhī mù
合 抱 之 木 ，

shēng yú háo mò
生 於 毫 末 ；

jiǔ céng zhī tái
九 層 之 臺 ，

qǐ yú lěi tǔ
起 於 累 土 ；

Chapter 64

A stable situation is easy to be maintained;

A condition without the sign of apparent change

　　is easy to be coped with;

A fragile thing is easy to break;

A minute thing is easy to dissolve.

The proper treatment should be prescribed

　　for what will happen;

Keep things in order before disorder sets in.

A huge tree grows from a tiny seedling;

A nine-storey terrace

　　rises from a mound of earth;

qiān lǐ zhī xíng
千里之行，

shǐ yú zú xià
始於足下。

wéi zhě bài zhī
爲者敗之；

zhí zhě shī zhī
執者失之。

shì yǐ　shèng rén
是以，聖人

wú wéi　gù wú bài
無爲，故無敗；

wú zhí　gù wú shī
無執，故無失。

mín zhī cóng shì
民之從事，

cháng yú jī chéng ér bài zhī
常於幾成而敗之。

shèn zhōng rú shǐ
慎終如始，*

zé wú bài shì
則無敗事。

＊郭店楚簡：臨事之紀，

A journey of a thousand *li*

    starts from beneath one's feet.

Those who want to obtain it

    by force will ruin it;

Those who hold it by force will lose it.

Thus the sage never ruins anything,

Because of his inaction;

He never loses anything,

Because he holds nothing.

In doing things,

People often fail on the verge of success.

If they are as prudent at the end

    as at the beginning,*

They will never fail.

---

* Guodian Chu Slips: The principle of handling a variety of affairs.

shì yǐ shèng rén yù bù yù
是以聖人欲不欲，

bù guì nán dé zhī huò
不貴難得之貨；

xué bù xué
學不學，**

fù zhòng rén zhī suǒ guò
復衆人之所過。***

yǐ fǔ wàn wù zhī zì rán ér bù gǎn wéi
以輔萬物之自然而不敢爲。

** 郭店楚簡：教不教，
*** 郭店楚簡：複衆人之所過。
辜按：與佛家"恒順衆生"意相通。(參閱49章)

That is why the sage

Desires what others do not desire,

Values not rare goods;

Learns what others do not learn**

Makes up for people's faults.***

In this way he helps all things develop

      naturally

And refrains from interfering in them.

**　Guodian Chu Slips: Teaches what others do not teach

***　Guodian Chu Slips: Follow the track of people.

Translator's note: The idea seems resembling to that of Budda, that is, always following the will of all sentients. (Cf. Chapter 49.)

六十五章

gǔ zhī shàn wéi dào zhě
古之善爲道者，

fēi yǐ míng mín
非以明民，

jiāng yǐ yú zhī
將以愚之。

mín zhī nán zhì
民之難治，

yǐ qí zhì duō
以其智多。

gù yǐ zhì zhì guó
故以智治國，

guó zhī zéi
國之賊；

bù yǐ zhì zhì guó
不以智治國，

guó zhī fú
國之福。

zhī cǐ liǎng zhě yì jī shì
知此兩者亦稽式。

cháng zhī jī shì
常知稽式，

shì wèi xuán dé
是謂玄德。

xuán dé shēn yǐ   yuǎn yǐ
玄德深矣，遠矣，

yǔ wù fǎn yǐ
與物反矣。

rán hòu nǎi zhì dà shùn
然後乃至大順。

Chapter 65

Those ancient men of the profound Tao
Did not use Tao to enlighten the people
But used Tao to make them simple.
The people are unruly
Because they are too clever.
Thus to govern a state by cleverness
Is bound to ruin the state;
Not to govern the state by cleverness
Is a blessing to the state.
These are two models of government;
Keeping the knowledge of these two models
Is known as the mysterious virtue.
The mysterious virtue is profound
    and far-reaching,
Running counter to concrete things.
At their extremes there is the most complete
    conformity to nature.

六十六章

jiāng hǎi suǒ yǐ néng wéi bǎi gǔ wáng zhě
江海所以能爲百谷王者，

yǐ qí shàn xià zhī
以其善下之，

gù néng wéi bǎi gǔ wáng
故能爲百谷王。

shì yǐ
是以

yù shàng mín
欲上民，

bì yǐ yán xià zhī
必以言下之；

yù xiān mín
欲先民，

bì yǐ shēn hòu zhī
必以身後之。

shì yǐ shèng rén
是以聖人

chǔ shàng ér mín bù zhòng
處上而民不重；

chǔ qián ér mín bù hài
處前而民不害。

shì yǐ tiān xià lè tuī ér bù yàn
是以天下樂推而不厭。

yǐ qí bù zhēng
以其不争，

gù tiān xià mò néng yǔ zhī zhēng
故天下莫能與之争。

Chapter 66

All the streamlets flow towards
　　the river and the sea
Because the latter takes the lower position,
Hence the latter becomes the king
　　of countless valleys.
Therefore, if one wants to be the ruler
　　of the people,
One must put oneself behind the people.
Thus the sage, though being placed
　　high over the people,
Never burdens the people;
The sage, though going
　　ahead of the people,
Never stands in the way of the people.
That is why the people hold him in esteem
And are never tired of him.
He contends with no one,
So no one in the world is able
　　to contend with him.

六十七章

tiān xià jiē wèi wǒ dào dà
天 下 皆 謂 我 道 大 ，

sì bù xiào
似 不 肖 。

fú wéi dà　gù sì bù xiào
夫 唯 大 ， 故 似 不 肖 。

ruò xiào
若 肖 ，

jiǔ yǐ qí xì yě fū
久 矣 其 細 也 夫 ！

wǒ yǒu sān bǎo　chí ér bǎo zhī
我 有 三 寶 ， 持 而 保 之 ：

yī yuē cí
一 曰 慈 ，

èr yuē jiǎn
二 曰 儉 ，

sān yuē bù gǎn wéi tiān xià xiān
三 曰 不 敢 爲 天 下 先 。

Chapter 67

The whole world says
  that my Tao is great,
Resembling nothing concrete.
Resembling nothing concrete,
Just because it is great.
If it resembled anything concrete,
It would have long become minute.
I have three most valuable things
Which I hold and treasure:
The first is mercy;
The second is thrift;
The third is unwillingness to take the lead
  in the world.

慈，故能勇，
cí　　gù néng yǒng

俭，故能　廣，
jiǎn　　gù néng guǎng

不敢爲天下先，故能　成器長。
bù gǎn wéi tiān xià xiān　　gù néng chéng qì zhǎng

今捨慈且勇，
jīn shě cí qiě yǒng

捨俭且廣，
shě jiǎn qiě guǎng

捨後且先，
shě hòu qiě xiān

死矣。
sǐ yǐ

夫慈，
fú cí

以戰則勝，
yǐ zhàn zé shèng

以守則固。
yǐ shǒu zé gù

天　將　救之，以慈衛之。
tiān jiāng jiù zhī　　yǐ cí wèi zhī

Being merciful, one can be brave;

Being thrifty, one can be generous;

Being unwilling to take the lead in the world,

One can become the leader of the world.

Now seeking bravery by giving up mercy,

Seeking generosity by giving up thrift,

Seeking advance by giving up retreat,

One is bound to end in death.

Being merciful,

    one will triumph in the offensive

And be impregnable in defense.

If heaven wants to save one,

It must save him with mercy.

六十八章

shàn wéi shì zhě bù wǔ
善 爲 士 者 不 武 ；

shàn zhàn zhě bù nù
善 戰 者 不 怒 ；

shàn shèng dí zhě bù yǔ
善 勝 敵 者 不 與 ；

shàn yòng rén zhě wéi zhī xià
善 用 人 者 爲 之 下 。

shì wèi bù zhēng zhī dé
是 謂 不 爭 之 德 ，

shì wèi yòng rén zhī lì
是 謂 用 人 之 力 ，

shì wèi pèi tiān
是 謂 配 天 ，

gǔ zhī jí
古 之 極 。

Chapter 68

He who is good at being a commander
Does not display his bravery;
He who is good at fighting
Does not burst into anger;
He who is good at defeating his enemy
Does not brace himself for a tough battle;
He who is good at employing men
Humbles himself before them;
This is called the virtue of non-contention;
This is called making use of others' strength;
This is called conformability
　　　to the Tao of heaven.

六十九章

yòng bīng yǒu yán
用兵有言：
　wú bù gǎn wéi zhǔ ér wéi kè
"吾不敢爲主而爲客，
bù gǎn jìn cùn ér tuì chǐ
不敢進寸而退尺。"
shì wèi
是謂
háng wú háng
行無行，
rǎng wú bì
攘無臂，
rēng wú dí
扔無敵，
zhí wú bīng
執無兵。
huò mò dà yú qīng dí
禍莫大於輕敵，
qīng dí jǐ sàng wú bǎo
輕敵幾喪吾寶。
gù kàng bīng xiāng jiā
故抗兵相加，
āi zhě shèng yǐ
哀者勝矣。

Chapter 69

A strategist says:

I dare not launch an attack

    but strengthen defense capabilities;

I dare not advance an inch

    but retreat a foot instead.

This means to deploy battle array

    by showing no battle array;

To wield one's arm to attack

    by showing no arm to lift;

To face the enemy

    by showing no enemy to attack;

To hold weapons

    by showing no weapons to hold.

No disaster is greater

    than underestimating the enemy.

Underestimating the enemy

    nearly cost me my treasure

    (i.e. three treasured valuable things.

    see Ch. 67).

That is why the sorrow-laden side wins

When two armies are at war.

七十章

wú yán shèn yì zhī
吾言甚易知，

shèn yì xíng
　甚易行。

tiān xià mò néng zhī
天下莫能知，

mò néng xíng
　莫能行。

yán yǒu zōng
言有宗，

shì yǒu jūn
事有君。

fú wéi wú zhī
夫唯無知，

shì yǐ bù wǒ zhī
是以不我知。

zhī wǒ zhě xī
知我者希，

zé wǒ zhě guì
則我者貴。

shì yǐ shèng rén
是以聖人

pī hè ér huái yù
　被褐而懷玉。

Chapter 70

My words are very easy to understand,
And very easy to be put into practice,
Yet there should have been no one
    in the world
Who can understand them
Or can put them into practice.
Words must be purpose-oriented,
Deeds must be reasonably grounded,
People cannot understand me
Because they fail to understand
    what is said above.
Those who understand me are few;
Those who can follow my advice
    are even less.
That is why the sage
Is always dressed in coarse cloth
But conceals about him
    a beautiful piece of jade (Tao).

七十一章

zhī bù zhī
知不知，

shàng yǐ
尚矣；

bù zhī zhī
不知知，

bìng yě
病也。

shèng rén bù bìng
聖人不病，

yǐ qí bìng bìng
以其病病，

fū wéi bìng bìng
夫惟病病，

shì yǐ bù bìng
是以不病。

Chapter 71

Knowing one's ignorance
　　of certain knowledge
　　is the best attitude；
Not knowing certain knowledge
　　yet pretending to know
　　is a bad attitude.
The sage is of no shortcoming，
Because he considers shortcoming
　　as shortcoming.
He considers shortcoming
　　as shortcoming，
Thus he has no shortcoming.

七十二章

民不畏威，
mín bù wèi wēi

　　則大威至。
　　zé dá wēi zhì

無狎其所居，
wú xiá qí suǒ jū

無厭其所生。
wú yàn qí suǒ shēng

夫唯不厭，
fú wéi bù yàn

是以不厭。
shì yǐ bù yàn

是以聖人
shì yǐ shèng rén

自知不自見，
zì zhī bù zì xiàn

自愛不自貴。
zì ài bù zì guì

故去彼取此。
gù qù bǐ qǔ cǐ

Chapter 72

When the people are not afraid of
    the threatening might of the authority,
The great tumult will soon ensue.
Do not harass their living places;
Do not deprive them of their means
    of livelihood.
If you do not oppress the people,
The people will not be tired of you
    (the ruler).
Hence the sage knows himself
    but does not praise himself;
Loves himself
    but does not honor himself.
That is why he discards the latter
    and takes the former.

七十三章

yǒng yú gǎn　　zé shā
勇於敢，則殺，

yǒng yú bù gǎn　　zé huó
勇於不敢，則活。

cǐ liǎng zhě huò lì huò hài
此兩者或利或害。

tiān zhī suǒ wù
天之所惡，

shú zhī qí gù
孰知其故？

shì yǐ shèng rén yóu nán zhī
是以聖人猶難之。

tiān zhī dào
天之道

bù zhēng ér shàn shèng
不爭而善勝，

bù yán ér shàn yìng
不言而善應，

bù zhào ér zì lái
不召而自來，

chǎn rán ér shàn móu
繟然而善謀。

tiān wǎng huī huī
天網恢恢，

shū ér bù shī
疏而不失。

Chapter 73

Bravery in being bold leads to death;

Bravery in being timid leads to life.

These two kinds of bravery,

One leads to good the other to harm.

Who knows why

Heaven hates what it hates?

Even the sage feels it difficult

    to understand.

This is the Tao of heaven:

To excel in triumphing

    by means of non-contention;

To be good at answering

    by means of taciturnity;

To attract people

    by using no summons;

To be quick in planning

    by acting slowly.

The net of heaven is spread wide and far,

Though the mesh is largely knit,

Nothing can slip through the net.

七十四章

mín bù wèi sǐ
民不畏死，

nài hé yǐ sǐ jù zhī
奈何以死懼之？

ruò shǐ mín cháng wèi sǐ
若使民常畏死，

ér wèi qí zhě
而爲奇者，

wú dé zhí ér shā zhī
吾得執而殺之。

shú gǎn
孰敢？

cháng yǒu sī shā zhě shā
常有司殺者殺。

fú dài sī shā zhě shā
夫代司殺者殺，

shì wèi dài dà jiàng zhuó
是謂代大匠斲。

fū dài dà jiàng zhuó
夫代大匠斲，

xī yǒu bù shāng qí shǒu zhě yǐ
希有不傷其手者矣。

Chapter 74

When the people are not afraid of death,
What is the point of threatening them
    with death?
Should the people really fear death,
Who dare go against laws
If we put to death those who do evils?
It is the duty of a regular executioner
    to kill,
If one wants to kill on behalf
    of the executioner,
It is like chopping wood
    on behalf of the master carpenter.
There are few who can escape
    cutting their own hands
When they chop wood
    on behalf of the master carpenter.

七十五章

mín zhī jī
民之饑，

yǐ qí shàng shí shuì zhī duō
以其上食税之多，

shì yǐ jī
是以饑。

mín zhī nán zhì
民之難治，

yǐ qí shàng zhī yǒu wéi
以其上之有爲，

shì yǐ nán zhì
是以難治。

mín zhī qīng sǐ
民之輕死，

yǐ qí shàng qiú shēng zhī hòu
以其上求生之厚，

shì yǐ qīng sǐ
是以輕死。

fú wéi wú yǐ shēng wéi zhě
夫唯無以生爲者，

shì xián yú guì shēng
是賢於貴生。

Chapter 75

The hunger on the part of the people

Is the result of exorbitant taxes

    on the part of the ruler;

Thus the people are hungry.

The unruliness on the part of the people

Is the result of meddlesome actions

    on the part of the ruler;

Thus the people are unruly.

Making light of life on the part of the people

Is the result of setting too much store by life

    on the part of the ruler;

Thus the people make light of life.

Those who make light of their own life.

Are wiser than those who overvalue their life.

七十六章

rén zhī shēng yě róu ruò
人 之 生 也 柔 弱，

qí sǐ yě jiān qiáng
其 死 也 坚 强 。

cǎo mù zhī shēng yě róu cuì
草 木 之 生 也 柔 脆，

qí sǐ yě kū gǎo
其 死 也 枯 槁 。

gù
故

jiān qiáng zhě sǐ zhī tú
坚 强 者 死 之 徒，

róu ruò zhě shēng zhī tú
柔 弱 者 生 之 徒 。

shì yǐ
是 以

bīng qiáng zé miè
兵 强 则 灭，

mù qiáng zé zhé
木 强 则 折 。

jiān qiáng chǔ xià
坚 强 处 下，

róu ruò chǔ shàng
柔 弱 处 上 。

Chapter 76

While alive, a man's body is supple;

When dead, it becomes hard.

While alive, grass and trees are supple,

When dead, they become dry and stiff.

Thus the hard and strong is of the dying sort;

The supple and weak is of the living sort.

That is why the army, having grown strong,

    will be wiped out,

And the tree, when grown up,

    will be cut down.

Thus the strong and big is inferior

To the weak and supple.

七十七章

tiān zhī dào
天之道，

　　qí yóu zhāng gōng yú
　　其猶張弓歟？

gāo zhě yì zhī
高者抑之，

xià zhě jǔ zhī
下者舉之，

yǒu yú zhě sǔn zhī
有餘者損之，

bù zú zhě bǔ zhī
不足者補之。

tiān zhī dào
天之道

sǔn yǒu yú ér bǔ bù zú
損有餘而補不足，

rén zhī dào zé bù rán
人之道則不然，

sǔn bù zú yǐ fèng yǒu yú
損不足以奉有餘。

shú néng yǒu yú yǐ fèng tiān xià
孰能有餘以奉天下？

wéi yǒu dào zhě
唯有道者。

shì yǐ shèng rén
是以聖人

wéi ér bù shì
爲而不恃，

gōng chéng ér bù chǔ
功成而不處，

qí bù yù xiàn xián
其不欲見賢。

Chapter 77

Does not the Tao of heaven
    resemble the bending of a bow
(aiming):
Pressing down the high,
Lifting up the low,
Reducing the excessive,
Compensating the deficient?
So the Tao of heaven means to compensate
    the deficient by reducing the excess.
The Tao of man is different:
It gives to one
    who already has more than enough
    by taking from one who is in want.
Who can offer what he has
    in excess to the people?
Only the man of Tao.

Thus the sage
Benefits all things without claiming
    to be their benefactor;
Succeeds without claiming credit;
Because he does not want
    to show off his wisdom.

七十八章

tiān xià mò róu ruò yú shuǐ
天 下 莫 柔 弱 於 水 ，

ér gōng jiān qiáng zhě mò zhī néng shèng
而 攻 堅 强 者 莫 之 能 勝 ，

qí wú yǐ yì zhī
其 無 以 易 之 。

ruò zhī shèng qiáng
弱 之 勝 强 ，

róu zhī shèng gāng
柔 之 勝 剛 ，

tiān xià mò bù zhī
天 下 莫 不 知 ，

mò néng xíng
莫 能 行 。

shì yǐ shèng rén yún
是 以 聖 人 云 ：

shòu guó zhī gòu
受 國 之 垢 ，

shì wèi shè jì zhǔ
是 謂 社 稷 主 ；

shòu guó bù xiáng
受 國 不 祥 ，

shì wèi tiān xià wáng
是 爲 天 下 王 。

zhèng yán ruò fǎn
正 言 若 反 。

Chapter 78

Nothing in the world is more supple
    than water,
Yet nothing is more powerful
    than water
    in attacking the hard and strong.
Why? Because nothing can take its place.
Everyone in the world knows
That the weak is more powerful
    than the strong,
That the supple is more rigid
    than the hard,
Yet no one so far
    can put the knowledge into practice.
That is why the sage says,
Only he who can bear the humiliation
    on behalf of the state
Can be called the great priest of the state;
Only he who dare shoulder the responsibility
    for the calamity of the state
Can be called the king of the state.
Factual words seem ironic.

七十九章

hé dà yuàn　　bì yǒu yú yuàn
和大怨，必有餘怨，

bào yuàn yǐ dé
報怨以德，

ān kě yǐ wéi shàn
安可以爲善？

shì yǐ shèng rén zhí zuǒ qì
是以聖人執左契

ér bù zé yú rén
而不責於人。

yǒu dé sī qì
有德司契，

wú dé sī chè
無德司徹。

tiān dào wú qīn
天道無親，

cháng yǔ shàn rén
常與善人。

道 德 经

Chapter 79

When the great enmity is allayed,

There must be some remaining hostility;

Even if one requites hostility with kindness,

How can that be considered perfect?

Therefore the sage keeps the stub

    of the receipt for a loan

But never presses for payment from people.

A man of virtue is as tolerant as the sage

    who keeps the stub of the receipt;

A man of no virtue is as harsh

    as tax collectors.

The Tao of heaven

    never shows favouritism;

It always helps those who are good.

二
二
三

八十章

xiǎo guó guǎ mín
小 國 寡 民 。

shǐ yǒu shí bǎi zhī qì ér bù yòng
使 有 什 伯 之 器 而 不 用 ；

shǐ mín zhòng sǐ ér bù yuǎn xǐ
使 民 重 死 而 不 遠 徙 ；

suī yǒu zhōu yú
雖 有 舟 與 ，

wú suǒ chéng zhī
無 所 乘 之 ；

suī yǒu jiǎ bīng
雖 有 甲 兵 ，

wú suǒ chén zhī
無 所 陳 之 。

shǐ rén fù jié shéng ér yòng zhī
使 人 復 結 繩 而 用 之 。

Chapter 80

The state should be small;

The population should be sparse.*

Tools, though of many kinds,

Should not be used.

Teach the people to fear death

And not to migrate to remote places;

Although they have ships and carts,

They will have no need to use them;

Although they are well armed

   with weapons,

They will have no place

   to make them effective.

Encourage the people

   to return to the condition

Under which the knotted rope was used

   to record things.

---

* Some scholars like Guo Shiming argues that the idea embodied in these two lines just runs counter to Lao Zi's true intention. See Guo Shiming, *What does Lao Zi Tell us After All*? Beijing: Hua Wen Press, 1999. p.332–336.

zhì zhì zhī jí
至治之極，

gān qí shí
甘其食，

měi qí fú
美其服，

ān qí jū
安其居，

lè qí sú
樂其俗，

lín guó xiāng wàng
鄰國相望，

jī quǎn zhī shēng xiāng wén
鷄犬之聲相聞，

mín zhì lǎo sǐ　　bù xiāng wǎng lái
民至老死，不相往來。

The world best ruled
    is a place where
The people will have delicious food,
    beautiful clothes,
    comfortable living quarters,
    cheerful customs.
Though within easy reach
    of neighbouring states,
The dog's barking
    and the cock's crowing
    in one state are heard in another;
The people of one state
    will never have dealings
    with those of another,
Even if they get old and die.

八十一章

xìn yán bù měi
信 言 不 美 ，

měi yán bù xìn
美 言 不 信 。

shàn zhě bù biàn
善 者 不 辩 ，

biàn zhě bù shàn
辩 者 不 善 。

zhì zhě bù bó
知 者 不 博 ，

bó zhě bù zhì
博 者 不 知 。

shèng rén bù jī
聖 人 不 積 ，

jì yǐ wéi rén jǐ yù yǒu
既 以 爲 人 己 愈 有 ，

jì yǐ yǔ rén yǐ yù duō
既 以 與 人 己 愈 多 。

tiān zhī dào
天 之 道 ，

lì ér bù hài
利 而 不 害 。

shèng rén zhī dào
聖 人 之 道 ，

wéi ér bù zhēng
爲 而 不 争 。

Chapter 81

True words are not embellished,
The embellished words are not true.
A good man does not quibble;
He who quibbles is not good.
A man of true learning does not
    show off his learning;
He who shows off his learning
    does not have true learning.
The sage does not store up.
Helping others as best as he can,
He is helped even more.
Giving others as much as he can,
He becomes richer and richer still.
The Tao of heaven benefits
    rather than harms all things;
The Tao of the sage is to give
    rather than rob the people.

郭店楚简《太一生水》

卷一

tài yī shēng shuǐ
太 一 生 水，

shuǐ fǎn fǔ tài yī
水 反 辅 太 一，

shì yǐ chéng tiān
是 以 成 天。

tiān fǎn fǔ tài yī
天 反 辅 太 一，

shì yǐ chéng dì
是 以 成 地。

tiān dì fù xiāng fǔ yě
天 地【復 相 辅】也，

shì yǐ chéng shén míng
是 以 成 神 明。

The Guodian Bamboo Slip Text:
The Great One Begot Water

Part I

The Great One Begot Water,

Water in turn assisted the Great One,

Thus Heaven took shape.

Heaven in turn assisted the Great One,

Thus Earth took shape.

Heaven and Earth in turn assisted each other,

Thus divinities appeared.

shén míng fù xiāng fǔ yě
神 明 復 相 輔 也 ，

shì yǐ chéng yīn yáng
是 以 成 陰 陽 。

yīn yáng fù xiāng fǔ yě
陰 陽 復 相 輔 也 ，

shì yǐ chéng sì shí
是 以 成 四 時 。

sì shí fù xiāng fǔ yě
四 時 復 ［ 相 ］ 輔 也 ，

shì yǐ chéng cāng rè
是 以 成 滄 熱 。

cāng rè fù xiāng fǔ yě
滄 熱 復 相 輔 也 。

shì yǐ chéng shī zǎo
是 以 成 濕 澡 。

shī zǎo fù xiāng fǔ yě
濕 澡 復 相 輔 也 ，

chéng suì ér zhǐ
成 歲 而 止 。

gù suì zhě
故 歲 者 ，

shī zǎo zhī suǒ shēng yě
濕 澡 之 所 生 也 。

shī zǎo zhě
濕 澡 者 ，

二 三 二

Divinities in turn assisted each other,
Thus *Yin* and *Yang* came into being.
Yin and *Yang* in turn assisted each other,
Thus the four seasons occurred.
The four seasons in turn assisted (each other),
Thus cold and heat were formed.
Cold and heat in turn assisted each other,
Thus there occurred humidity and dryness.
Humidity and dryness in turn assisted each other,
Thus we have the period called the year.
Therefore, the year
Was generated by humidity and dryness;
Humidity and dryness

cāng rè zhī suǒ shēng yě
滄 熱 之 所 生 也。

cāng rè zhě
滄 熱 者,

sì shí zhī suǒ shēng yě
【四 時 之 所 生 也】,

sì shí zhě
四 時 者

yīn yáng zhī suǒ shēng yě
陰 陽 之 所 生 也。

yīn yáng zhě
陰 陽 者,

shén míng zhī suǒ shēng yě
神 明 之 所 生 也。*

shén míng zhě
神 明 者,

tiān dì zhī suǒ shēng yě
天［地］之 所 生 也。

tiān dì zhě
天 地 者,

dà yī zhī suǒ shēng yě
大 一 之 所 生 也。

shì gù dà yī
是 故 大 一

---

* 一般学者理解为天神、地祇。我以为据上下文意,"神明"更像指光明与阴暗两种状态。

Were generated by cold and heat.

Cold and heat

Were generated by the four seasons.

And the four seasons

Were generated by *Yin* and *Yang*.

Yin and *Yang*

Were generated by darkness and brightness. *

Darkness and brightness

Were generated by Heaven [and Earth].

And Heaven and Earth

Were generated by the Great One.

Thus, the Great One

---

* Scholars interpret 神明 as divinities. I am inclined to understand the word from the context as two phenomena: brightness (from the sun and the moon) and darkness (from the earth).

cáng yú shuǐ
藏 於 水 ，

xíng yú shí
行 於 時 。

zhōu ér huò shǐ
周 而 或 【始】，

yǐ jǐ wéi wàn wù mǔ
【以已爲】萬勿母 。

yī quē yī yíng
一 缺 一 盈 ，

yǐ jǐ wéi wàn wù jīng
以 已 爲 萬 勿 經 。

cǐ tiān zhī suǒ bù néng shā
此 天 之 所 不 能 殺 ，

dì zhī suǒ bù néng lí
地 之 所 不 能 厘 ，

yīn yáng zhī suǒ bù néng chéng
陰 陽 之 所 不 能 成 。

jūn zǐ zhī cǐ zhī wèi tài yī
君 子 知 此 之 胃 【太一】**
□□□□□□□□ 。

** 君子知此之胃[太一]: 有的学者认为这里的缺字应该是"圣人"或"道"。虽然也有道理。但我个人更倾向于缺字指的是"太一"，以照应篇首的"太一生水"。

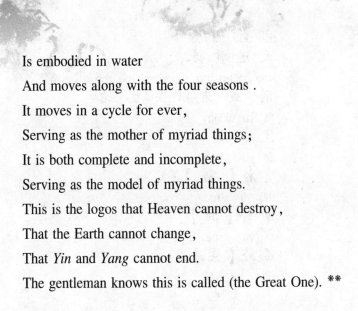

Is embodied in water

And moves along with the four seasons .

It moves in a cycle for ever,

Serving as the mother of myriad things;

It is both complete and incomplete,

Serving as the model of myriad things.

This is the logos that Heaven cannot destroy,

That the Earth cannot change,

That *Yin* and *Yang* cannot end.

The gentleman knows this is called (the Great One). **

** Some scholars conjecture the missing words could be "the sage" or "the way". I deem their interpretations reasonable but I myself feel more like to think the missing part is "the Great One" so as to correspond to the opening statement of the text: "The Great One Begot Water".

卷二

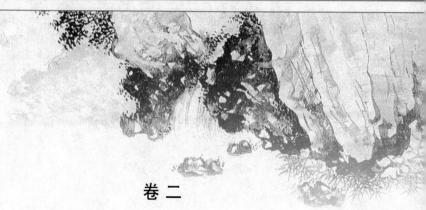

tiān dào guì ruò
天 道 贵 弱，

xiāo chéng zhě yǐ yì shēng zhě
削 成 者 以 益 生 者，

fá yú qiáng
伐 於 强，

zé yú　　gāng
责 於【刚】；

zhù yú　　ruò
助 於【弱】，

yì yú　 róu
益 於【柔】。

xià　　tǔ yě
下 ，土 也，

ér wèi zhī dì
而 胃 之 地。

shàng　　qì yě
上 ，气 也，

ér wèi zhī tiān
而 胃 之 天。

Part II

The Tao of Heaven values the weak,

It weakens the successful so as to benefit the living;

It attacks the strong;

It punishes[the rigid];

It helps [the weak];

It benefits [the gentle].

What is beneath our feet is soil;

We call it the Earth;

What is above our heads is air;

We call it Heaven.

dào yì qí zì yě
道 亦 其 字 也 。***

qǐng wèn qí míng
請 問 其 名

yǐ dào cóng shì zhě
以 道 從 事 者 ，

bì tuō qí míng
必 托 其 名 ，

gǔ shì chéng ér shēn cháng
古 事 成 而 身 長 ；

shèng rén zhī cóng shì yě
聖 人 之 從 事 也 ，

yì tuō qí míng
亦 托 其 名 ，

gù gōng chéng ér shēn bù tì
故 功 成 而 身 不 剔 。

tiān dì míng chèng bìng lì
天 地 名 稱 並 立 ，

gū guò qí fāng
姑 過 其 方 ，

bù sī xiāng dāng
不 思 相 【 當 】 。

tiān bù zú yú xī běi
【 天 不 足 】 於 西 北 ，

*** 即头与脚;天与地。

Likewise, Tao is just what the word *Dao* (道) itself

    means.***

Then what does the name of Tao mean?

He who does his business by using Tao

Must do it in the name of Heaven and Earth (Tao),

That's why he can have a successful career and good health.

When the Sage does his work,

He does it in the same name of Heaven and Earth,

Thus he succeeds without harming himself.

Both as the signifiers and the signified, Heave and Earth

Are just named as expedients,

They are not to be thought of as things 【equal】.

［Heaven is low］in the northwest,

＊＊＊That is, the head and feet; the Heaven and Earth.

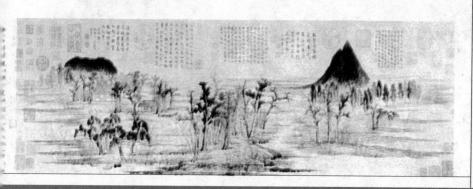

其下高以强。
qí xià gāo yǐ qiáng

地不足於東南，
dì bù zú yú dōng nán

其上【高以强】。
qí shàng gāo yǐ qiáng

【不足於上】者，
bù zú yú shàng zhě

又餘於下；
yòu yú yú xià

不足於下者，
bù zú yú xià zhě

又餘於上。
yòu yú yú shàng

二四二

But is high and strong in the southeast.

The earth is thin in the southeast,

But is [high and strong] in the northwest.

[i.e. that which does not have enough in the northwest]

Has more than enough in the southeast;

That which does not have enough in the southeast

Has more than enough in the northwest.

Bibliography

郭店楚简国际学术研讨会论文集

馬王堆漢墓帛書老子

河上公　老子章句

河上公　道德真經注

河上公　老子道德經章句　葛玄造序

嚴　遵　道德真經指歸　舊題漢嚴君平撰

王　弼　老子注

王　弼　道德真經注

王　弼　老子道德經注　侯官嚴復評點

傅　奕　道德經古本篇

傅　奕　校定古本老子

唐玄宗　御注道德真經

唐玄宗　御製道德真經疏

羅振玉　道德經考異及老子考異補遺

李　約　老子道德真經新注

陸希聲　道德真經傳

强思齊　道德真經玄德纂疏

王　真　道德真經論兵要義述

成玄英　道德經義疏

張君相　道德真經注疏　舊題為吳徵士顧歡述

(唐)李榮　老子道德經注

杜光庭　道德真經廣聖義

陸德明　經典釋文

陳景元　道德真經藏室纂微篇

宋徽宗　御解道德真經

范應元　老子道德經古本集注

陳象古　道德真經解

呂惠卿　道德真經傳

邵若愚　道德真經直解

司馬光　道德真經論

王安石　老子注(容肇祖輯)

蘇　轍　道德真經注

林希逸　道德真經口義

董思靖　道德真經集解

李　霖　道德真經取善集

彭　耜　道德真經繫注

趙至堅　道德真經疏義

(宋)李榮　道德真經疏義

呂知常　道德經講義

寇才質　道德真經四子古道集解

趙秉文　道德真經集解

杜道堅　道德玄經原旨

吳　澄　道德真經注

劉惟永　道德真經集義

明太祖　御注道德真經

危大有　道德經集義

周如砥　道德經解集義

白玉蟾　道德經妙門約

永樂大典本　老子

王夫之　老子衍

魏　源　老子本義

姚　鼐　老子章義

畢　沅　老子考異

俞　樾　老子平議　見諸子平議

孫詒讓　老子札記

陶紹學　校老子

譚　獻　讀老子

易順鼎　讀老子札記

陶鳴慶　讀老子札記(附：王弼注勘誤)見讀諸子札記

奚　侗　老子集解

朱芾煌　老子述異

馬叙倫　老子校詁

高　亨　老子正詁

勞　健　老子古本考

朱謙之　老子校釋

蔣錫昌　老子校詁

楊興順　中國古代哲學家老子及其學說

車　載　論老子

汪奠基　老子樸素辯證的邏輯思想——無名論

張起鈞　老子哲學

錢鍾書　老子王弼注　見管錐編第二册

詹劍峰　老子其人其書及其道論

陳鼓應　老子注譯及評介

張松如　老子校讀

李息齋　道德真經義解

王守正　道德真經衍義手鈔

李道純　道德會元

張嗣成　道德真經章句訓頌

魏　征　群書治要(老子)

白玉蟾　蟾仙解老

薛君采　老子集解

畢　沅　老子道德經考异

李　摯　老子解

張爾岐　老子説略

王念孫　老子雜志

陳　澧　老子注

羅連賢　老子餘誼

何仕驥　古本道德經校刊

高　明　帛書老子甲乙本與今本老子勘校札記

鄭樹良　論帛書老子

韓非子　解老喻老

陸德明　老子道德經音義

饒宗頤　老子想爾注校箋

蒙文通　成玄英老子義疏輯本

王　道　老子億

高延第　老子證義

陶鴻慶　讀老子札記

嚴　復　老子道德經評點

于　鬯　香草續校書

馬其昶　老子故

楊增新　補過齋讀老子日記

蔡廷幹　老解老

楊樹達　老子古義

王重民　老子考

陳　柱　老子集訓

馮　振　老子通證

張默生　老子章句新解

楊柳橋　老子譯話

于省吾　老子新證

周紹賢　老子要義

張舜徽　周秦道論發微

馮友蘭、任繼愈等　老子哲學討論集

張岱年　老子哲學辨微

胡哲敷　老莊哲學

張成秋　先秦道家思想研究

嚴靈峰　老莊研究

任繼愈　老子今譯

任繼愈　老子新譯

裘錫圭　郭店《老子》簡初探

郭世銘　《老子》究竟说什么

尹振环　楚简老子辨析

Sarah Allan & Crispin Williams, ed. *The Guodian Lao Zi: Proceedings of the Juternational Conference*, Dartmouth college, May 1998

彭浩　郭店楚简《老子》校读

崔仁义　荆门郭店楚简老子研究

郭沂　郭店楚简与先秦学术思想

李零　郭店楚简校读记

廖名春　郭店楚简老子校释

譯者簡介

辜正坤,北京大学英语系教授,博士研究生导师,获国务院政府特殊津贴证书,北京大学文化文学与翻译研究学会会长,兼任中国莎士比亚研究会副会长,中华民族文化促进会常务理事,法中文化艺术协会理事,美国名人传记研究院顾问,清华大学、南开大学、美国瓦西塔大学客座教授、北京东方神州书画院一级书画师及《世界文学与翻译研究》杂志主编。历获北京大学科研成果著作一等奖、北京市高校哲学社会科学优秀奖、全国首界中青年翻译理论优秀奖、全国图书金钥匙奖等。国际上曾获由美国传记研究院颁发的"二十一世纪成就奖"和"国际文化荣誉奖"。国画水墨荷花曾获1996中国芙蓉杯诗书画大奖赛优秀奖。有关辜正坤的传记已收入美国传记研究院编纂出版的《全球领先人物500名》(第3版)一书、英国剑桥《国际知识界名人录》(第11版)以及港中国际交流出版社出版的《世界名人录》(1997年版)等十多种辞书。辜正坤的主要著、译、编著作有《莎士比亚研究》(英文版)(巴黎莎士比亚同人社,香港,1993),《东西诗研究合璧论》(香港新世纪出版社,1993),《世界名诗鉴赏词典》(主编)(北京大学出版社,1990),《世界诗歌鉴赏大典》(上下卷)(主编)(台湾地球出版社,1992),《林肯文集》(下卷)(三联书店,北京,1993),《第三世纪》(人民

出版社,1990),《中国二十世纪纯抒情诗精华》(主编)(作家出版社,1990),《老子英译》(北京大学出版社,1995),《英国浪漫派散文精华》(主编)(作家出版社,1989),《毛泽东诗词译注》(英文版)(北京大学出版社,1993),《莎士比业十四行诗集》(北京大学出版社,1997;译林出版社,1997),《中国历代名诗300首评注》(主编)(北京出版社,1998),《外国名诗300首评注》(主编)(北京出版社,1998),《英文名篇鉴赏金亩》(诗歌卷、散文卷、戏剧卷主编)(天津人民出版社,1998),《未来之路》(北京大学出版社,1996),《中西诗比较鉴赏与翻译理论》(专著)(清华大学出版社,2003),《互构语言文化学原理》(专著)(清华大学出版社,2004),《元曲一百五十首》英译(北京大学出版社,2004),《译学津原》(专著)(文心出版社,2005),《古希腊文学史》,见《欧洲文学史》第一卷(国家85重点科研专案,商务印书馆,1999),《莎士比亚概论》, 见《欧洲文学史》第一卷 (国家85重点科研专案,商务印书馆,1999),《国际翻译学新探》(主编)(天津百花文艺出版社,2006),《莎士比亚十四行诗精选》(华文出版社,2006),等四十七部(种)作品。辜正坤曾为北京大学研究生讲授过中西文化比较、莎士比亚、诗歌、翻译理论与技巧、西方学术精华概论、英国文学史、古希腊、罗马文学史等课程。1993年应邀任联合国教科文总部(巴黎)翻译;曾在国内外用英汉两种文字发表过各类学术文章100余篇。现为国家社会科学十五重点科研项目"外国古代神话和史诗研究"主持人。

About the Translator

Gu Zhengkun, Ph.D., Professor of Comparative Culture and Translation at Peking University, President of Culture and Translation Society of Peking University, Council Member of National Culture Promotion Society of China, Council Member of National Translation Association of China, and Vice President of Shakespeare Association of China. He is also the winner of many honors and awards such as the First Prize for Academic Achievement awarded by the authority of Peking University (1991), Social Sciences Award for the Middle-aged College Teachers offered by the Educational Bureau of the City of Peking (1992), the National Translation Theory Prize (1989), the National

Gold Key Book Award (1991) and Special Government Grant awarded by the State Council for outstanding educational achievement (2002). He is the author and translator of 47 books. Of them the best known are *A Companion to Masterpieces in World poetry* (1990), *Lao Tzu: The Book of Tao and Teh* (in English, 1993), *150 Masterpieces in Yuan Qu-poetry* (in English, 2004), *Shakespeare's Sonnets* (in Chinese, 1995), *China and West: Comparative Poetics and Translatology* (2003), *Linguistic Culturology* (2004) and *Exploration into Translatology* (2005). He has also published more than 100 articles at home and abroad either in English or in Chinese. For the recent ten years he has been teaching Peking University undergraduates as well as doctoral students comparative culture, Shakespeare and translation: theory and skills. He worked in UNESCO(Paris) as well as in UN(Geneva) in 1993 and was guest professor of Tsinghua University, Nankai University and Wachita Baptist University, U.S.A. in 2001-2002.